TABLE OF CONTENTS

Ronin Books

*Everyone knows that
something is going to happen.
The seeds of the sixties have
taken root underground. The
blossoming is to come.*

POLITICS
OF
PSYCHO-
PHARMACOLOGY

Timothy Leary

Ronin Publishing
Berkeley, CA
roninpub.com

Politics of PsychoPharmacology
ISBN: 1-57951-056-6
Copyright © 1988 by Timothy Leary
Copyright © 2002 by Futique Trust

Published by
RONIN Publishing, Inc.
PO Box 522
Berkeley, CA 94701
roninpub.com

Credits:

Editor:	**Beverly A. Potter** docpotter.com
Cover Design:	**Judy July, Generic Type** generictype.com

Fonts:	Ariel Narrow Flowerchild by Marty Bee Gouty Hypnotica by Deniart

Distributed to the trade by **Publishers Group West**
Printed in the United States of America by **Bertelsmann**
Library of Congress Card Number: **2002101491**

Note: Material in the book was excerpted from *Changing My Mind Among
Others* (1988) by *Timothy Leary*.

RETrO
FLECTIONS

BY ALEXANDER SHULGIN

I HAVE OFTEN BEEN ASKED if I believed that Timothy Leary's very blatant public position concerning the open use of these remarkable drugs had helped bring the legal axe down upon them. I really don't believe so.

Oh, it was true that the newspaper reporters loved his outrageous press conferences, and he in turn loved the chance to reassert the mantra, "Turn on, tune in, drop out." But I feel that the primary force that led to the first laws against LSD and the companion psychedelics was a political one.

This book takes place at the time of the Vietnam War, and the Hippie Summer of Love in San Francisco that was seen as a vocal—and drug-related—protest against it. And since the ruling authorities couldn't easily move against the open protest and the accompanying Grateful Dead music in the fields of Golden Gate Park, they moved against the drugs that were being used.

At that time, the anti-drug law that was in effect was the Harrison Narcotics Act, which, in essence, covered three drugs. When it was first made into law in 1914 there were the opium relatives, including morphine and heroin, and coca relatives including cocaine. A third plant world was added through the Marihuana Tax Act of 1937, officially making marijuana—only the law spells it with an "h" —a "narcotic" in the eyes of the BN (Bureau of Narcotics).

We witnessed the "turn-on of the month" club.

Then the mid-sixties hit, with not only the broad popularization of LSD, but with what became know as the "turn-on of the month" club. There appeared new initials such as PCP, and MDA, and STP, and everyone was talking about—and using—mescaline and peyote.

Stepped Up Enforcement

It was obvious to Congress that these were not more narcotics, but something quite different. There was quickly established the BDAC (Bureau of Drug Abuse Control) and it was to be operated under the FDA (Food and Drug Administration) under the wing of the Department of Agriculture. The BN functioned under the Department of Treasury. All these new "non-narcotic" drugs were written into the BDAC law and there were two competing drug law-enforcing bodies. Actually three if you reckoned in the BATF (Bureau for Administration of Tobacco and Firearms).

Finally, in 1968, the two drug groups were spun together into a single unit, the BNDD (Bureau of Narcotics and Dangerous Drugs), that functioned under the Department of Justice. The passage of the Controlled Substance Act in 1970 superceded all of this and the DEA (Drug Enforcement Administration), formed in 1973, is still with us today.

AN Early Rave

I remember a fantastic conference that was arranged about that time. It was to cover all aspects of LSD and, of course, Tim Leary was to be a major participant. It was initially arranged to be held on the University of California campus in Berkeley. But there was a rapidly growing controversy among the faculty and the University administrators, that it might cast the University in a pro-drug image, which could be seen by some as synonymous with an anti-war position.

Large announcements were posted all around Berkeley and I remember seeing one with the words "Jew! Jew! Jew!" written with a heavy black pen defacing it. A decision was made to relocate the meeting to the U.C. Extension buildings on Laguna Street in San Francisco. But that wasn't the end of the conflict by any means. I, along with several of my research friends, happily bought attendance tickets and enjoyed all aspects of the show.

There must have been around 500 people present, and they were identified by their costumes. Most of us were loosely dressed in colorful shirts and blue jeans. But a small minority was in dark suits and wearing conservative ties, largely gathered over along the south wall of the auditorium. Most had cameras with flash attachments, and they photographed everything and everyone.

> **We figured the black suits with cameras were undercover cops.**

There was nothing subtle about them at all. And we who knew each other interacted with friends of our friends, and we all spent quite a bit of effort trying to determine just who the hippie-dressed characters were whom no one recognized; we speculated that they—at least some of them—might be undercover police.

THeY TrIeD TO MUZZLe GINSBerG

A major participant was the famous beat poet, Allen Ginsberg. I had the pleasure of seeing him in a verbal encounter with the then-current State Attorney General—whose name I think was Younger. Allen was jumping up and down in front of him shouting *"Eichmann! Eichmann! Eichmann!"* but there was no emotion or apparent recognition of the AG's face. He had been invited to be a speaker but sensed the ways things were going and decided no to address the group.

The show finally got underway, with a circle of interesting people on the stage. The Master of Ceremonies set the tone of the entire meeting by welcoming everyone with great warmth, to which the audience responded with shouts of *"Yea"* and much applause. Then he made an announcement that the University authorities had insisted that Allen Ginsberg not be allowed to address the audience. Boos sounded everywhere.

But then he invited Allen up to the stage, and said that he had no objection to his joining the group there and that he could make whatever comments he wished to from his new status as an observer rather than as a speaker. Cheers sounded everywhere.

In the evening, there was one of the very first light shows ever put on in public, and it gave introduction to Tim Leary, who addressed a completely packed adjacent auditorium with a great speech. The black suits had long since left and the party went on until the small hours—no one wanted to go home and the University monitors simply abandoned their effort at closing the place.

> **There are enthusiasts of the freedom of personal exploration and those who hold it illegal and immoral.**

Yes, there was a lot of psychopharmacology in evidence at that meeting. And a lot of politics apparent in its own way. All that was well over thirty years ago, but in a way the raves of today are the locale of this perennial interaction of the two opposite philosophies.

There are those who are the enthusiasts of the freedom of personal exploration, and those who hold that all such activity is both illegal and immoral. This eternal conflict is vividly apparent in this book by Timothy Leary, *The Politics of PsychoPharmacology*.

—Sasha Shulgin
author of
Pihkal: A Chemical Love Story
Tihkal: The Continuation
Controlled Substances

preface

※

BY TIMOTHY LEARY

I BEGAN MY CAREER as a scientist and gradually changed from theory and methodology to neuropolitics. Was this transition unexpected? Nope! A study of the history of science and philosophy is clear on this point. A successful Socratic scientific innovator who presents the species with a new technology for changing human nature and human destiny is *always* in trouble with the politicians. A philosopher who does his job well invariably upsets the hive and has to deal with the forces set up to preserve the old order and prevent change.

WHAT'S SO TABOO?

Why is the topic of drugs so taboo? Because the use of drugs is the first and the last frontier of human freedom. They give the individual the power to move his consciousness in any direction he desires; given control of his own nervous system, the individual essentially can become the kind of person he wants to become.

In his eloquent Afterword, Richard Glen Boire explains the force driving the taboo—regulation of consciousness. The government is mandated to maintain the status quo and that extends into the privacy of our thoughts and perceptions. Unauthorized mental states are not permitted!

The real revolution of the sixties was neurological.

Politics of PsychoPharmacology is a chronicle of how I learned this lesson— the hard way. I was hounded, shackled and imprisoned, like a common criminal, for experimenting with my consciousness—and suggesting that others do so as well. The persecution was unrelenting until I finally bowed to authority and told the "truth"—then they set me "free."

—Timothy Leary

from the other side

The courtroom is the worst forum for new ideas. Galileo lost. Giordano Bruno got the hot seat. Scopes lost in Tennessee defending evolution. The Jews and Italians threw the book at Jesus for preaching love while the crook Barabbas got off. There's a 2,000-year-old public relations lesson for philisophers there.

—Richard Alpert
aka. Ram Dass
quoted in *Flashbacks*

1

SEEDS OF THE SIXTIES

IN JANUARY, 1960 I accepted an invitation to go to Harvard to initiate new programs in what was then called "Behavior Change". I was convinced that drastic limitations on human intellectual and emotional function were caused by inflexible states of mind, static and conditioned neural circuits, which created and preserved malfunctional states of perceived reality. In the then—Zeitgeist of Salk, Fleming, Pauling, I believed that the right chemical used correctly was the cure. The "ailment" I had selected as curable was human nature.

> **Man did not know how to use his head.**

I believed that man did not know how to use his head, that the static, repetitive normal mind was itself the source of "dis-ease" and that the task was to discover the neuro-chemical for changing mind. Our initial experiments at Harvard suggested that LSD might be such a drug.

we Dw research

From our research offices at Harvard circa
1960 to 63 and later at Millbrook from 1963 to 68,
we conducted the largest voluntary psychosocial
experiment in history. Our hypotheses were simple.
History seemed to show that our human species has
always eagerly accepted any new technology that gave
us more power to receive and transmit information. Our
experiment sought to demonstrate that it is in our
nature to want to expand consciousness, change our
brains, open up to new experiences. Radio, television,
transistors, and psychoactive drugs are all instruments
for widening the range of input experience.

The role of human beings in the Gala life-web is
information processing. As the wave of civilization
moved westward during the last 4,000 years, the function, would do so. To test this hypothesis, we publicized
the Brain-Change Option and sat back to observe and
record the results.

We tested our hypotheses in a series of controlled
experiments; the setting or expectation for philosophic
exploration and self-discovery was supportive, secure,
and respectable. *There was not one casualty or "bad trip."*
Our subjects would routinely experience meta-mind
intensities and were encouraged to contemplate the
implications of these new signals

EVIDENCE

Clear-cut evidence emerged. Given the
opportunity, an overwhelming majority of

young people in the Western democratic societies bought the chance to activate their brains and dial-tune expanded reception. At first we were shocked to discover that the option to reimprint, to change, to fabricate new realities was not eagerly accepted by the adults who obviously needed it most. We were less surprised when we looked up a dictionary definition of the word "adult."

WHaT'S aN ADULT?

Past participle of the Latin verb adolescare, "to grow." The adult is that state of the individual, which will undergo no further metamorphosis or change. The adult is the rinal stage of over-specialization.

IMPLICaTIONS

The implications for human freedom were far-reaching. To describe this new science of precise, disciplined brain-change, I suggested the term *Neurologic*—the understanding and control of one's own nervous system. More important, the human being is seen as having several "minds"—defined as neural circuits—which evolve during the course of individual development and which can be turned on and off selectively.

In 1960-63 we experimented with drug-induced brain-change in prison rehabilitation, psychedelic psychotherapy, and personality change. The hypotheses were confirmed. We cut the prison-return rate by 90%.

We demonstrated quantitative psychometric improve-
ment in personality. It was prize-winning, elegant
research. Our subjects shared our enthusiasm, but the
medical directors didn't. We were surprised to discover
that many administrators didn't really want to eliminate the pathologies they administer.

Fear
of Change

God knows they liked me personally, re-
spected our results, and hoped that we were
right. But there is inertial fear of change. Three
times I was offered tenure at Harvard—and the post of
chief psychologist at Massachusetts
General Hospital—*if* I would just
play down the drug research. But
by then, we had entered that
ancient current of passionate hope
and risky belief that humanity can evolve into a higher
wisdom.

God knows they liked me but—

Each month, the results of our experiment flashed
across the nation. Gallup polls; alarmed government
statistics; worried college deans' warnings. The percentage of psychedelic-drug users consistently climbed, the
percentage of long-hairs rose. Rock-and-roll music kept
pushing the beat.

2

I BECAME AN ACTIVIST CHANGE AGENT

I LEFT Harvard IN 1963, abandoned the role of conventional, academic, scientist, and became, without knowing it, a shaman, and an activist change-agent. This shift was accomplished slowly, hesitantly, and with self-conscious humor. First, a diligent study of religious history revealed that psychedelic plants had been used in Egypt, Persia, India, China, and Greece—always for initiation into adulthood, entrance into the spiritual life, and for the training of prophets and special priests who played colorful, apparently necessary roles. At the same time I began personal training in Hindu Vedanta, Buddhist Tantra, and Taoist techniques for understanding the flow of various energies. The "obligatory pilgrimage" to India occurred.

Administrators didn't want to eliminate the pathologies they administered.

In 1963 we started centers for training in consciousness expansion, a scientific journal, and lecture tours for communicating the results of our research. Our Castalia Foundation was visited by musicians, electronic sound technicians, painters, and light technicians. The new modes of art we developed—based on the capacity of the nervous system to receive, synthesize, and transmit accelerated, compressed, and multimedia presentations—have since been taken over by commercial film and television people and have become commonplace at raves.

> Like artists, blacks and the young—psychedelic people lived closer to a pagan life of fleshy pleasure.

At this time the "new consciousness" became a political issue indissolubly intertwined with peace, sexual liberation, reform of education, racial equilibrium, ecology, and "end the draft." The love-ins, hippie beads, the Beatles, and the demonstrations were the froth. The real thing had to do with the way people looked each other in the eye and smiled, knowing that something new and self-responsible was happening in their heads. Messages came to us from the dissenting underground in Russia and Brazil. The real revolution of the sixties was neurological.

CHaNGe YOUR BraIN

Make up
Your Own Mind

I devoted my energies to establishing a
nonrepressive society by encouraging a large
group of young Americans to re-imprint themselves away from the work-duty conditioning, and get
back where they belong. Our hope was to bring about
change where all change must originate—in the brain.
The aim was to produce the first generation in history
to choose its own mode of imprint conditioning, react
selectively to self-selected rewards and, literally, make
up its own mind.

By the fall of 1965, to the despair of the law-and-
order generation, the young were joyously rejecting the
Protestant work ethic. Psychedelic people inevitably
became more and more like the artistic, the blacks, and
the young—those three outgroups who live closer to a
pagan life of natural fleshly pleasure.

The complex tasks of the new social structure now
could be left to the younger and more talented. Thus
honorably emeriti, my wife Rosemary and I turned
ourselves to post-retirement projects—to stay high,
make love, and write science fiction—or so we hoped.

3

BUSTED IN Laredo!

IN DECEMBER 1965, we closed the house at Millbrook and drove to Mexico, where we had rented a beach house. We got to Laredo, Texas, at sundown and drove across the International Bridge, and parked in front of the Immigration Building. But we weren't able to get our tourist cards. We were told to come back the next day. I sensed trouble. Jack and Rosemary cleaned out the car in the parking lot and flushed our small stash—just in case.

> "What is this seed, Dr. Leary!"

If we had stayed the night in Nuevo Laredo we wouldn't have had to go through Customs, but unthinking I drove to the International Bridge. Halfway across Rosemary remembered the grass in her little silver box. We worried that tossing it out the window would be seen so Susan hid it in her clothes.

OUTTa THE Car!

Even though we hadn't been in Mexico, we had to pass through American Customs. At the Customs station I handed the Officer our unused Mexican papers and explained that we hadn't entered Mexico. Ignoring me, the Customs Officer ordered everyone out of the car, leaned in the front door, reached down and came up with something in his fingers. "What is this seed I found on your car floor?" In a flash, the car was surrounded by agents.

They searched the suitcases, scuba gear, and my papers. Then we had to stip—they called in a matron for Rosemary and Susan. The little silver box was discovered, of course. "*Your daughter and wife are under arrest!*" the Customs Officer barked. "I'll take responsibility for the marijuana," I piped in, and with those words, I became a criminal.

REPENT or ROT N JaIL

If I assumed a repentant attitude, de-nounce drugs, and made a deal, advised my Laredo lawyer, I'd get four months in jail and probation. Indignant, "*Repent!*" I snorted. "*I was framed. I'm fighting this!*" "*Yeah! Yeah! I've heard this before. You won't win. You don't understand how it is here. This is not Harvard; this is South Texas,*" the lawyer explained.

"Just tell the truth," the lawyer continued, *"and you'll walk."* The grass was found on Susan and belonged to Rosemary, not to me. There was no case against me. All I had to do was to let my wife and daughter take the fall. The lawyer assurred me that they would get off easy. *"That's a cop-out! It's immoral!"*

"If you insist on taking responsibility for the marijuana," the lawyer said in exasperation, *"you'll go to jail for years. You don't realize how bad this can get."*

MOMENT OF POLITICAL TRUTH

How did I feel about being "made an example of"? I expressed it well in *Flashbacks*, my autobiography, published by Tarcher:

"Here it was. The moment of political truth. My Laredo lawyer said it: "They want to make an example of you." Well, I'd make an example of them...

"I wasn't going to submit passively to the role of scapegoat, the Harvard psychologist who got in that trouble over drugs. Liberty was at stake here, freedom of access to your own body and brain, a right I believed, was protected by the Constitution.

"Sutting in a dark jail cell on Christmas Eve 1965, flushed with virtuous indignation about the wickedness of the marijuana laws, I resolved to fight the case in the courts of the land , to mobilize legal teams, to devise courtroom tactics, to file appeals, motions, briefs, depositions, to speak in defense of the right of American citizens to manage their own bodies and brains.

The fatal word in this naive program was "fight." The adversary nature of the judicial process has never been favorable to philosophers and scientists. Would I choose this arena of battle again? I don't know. It was a stage I had to go through. And go through it I did."

The fatal word in this naive program was "fight."

I WAS MADE INTO AN EXAMPLE

The indictments came down in January. Susan and I were charged with smuggling marijuana, transporting marijuana, and failure to pay the marijuana tax. After the verdict, the Laredo judge sentenced me to 30 years' imprisonment and imposed a $30,000 fine for possessing half an ounce of grass. That was a whole lot of money in those days—enough to buy an upper-middle class home in California, for example—still is a whole lot of money.

Lost in the headlines was the uneasy knowledge that the Federal weed law viiolated the fifth Amendment forbidding self-incrimination by being forced to pay taxes for an illegal act.

4

INEVITABLE BACKLASH

THE INEVITABLE BACKLASH began in 1966 when various legislatures and Congress began considering bills to criminalize LSD and similar drugs. In that year I testified before two Senate committees, and my political position was by no means radical or solitary.

> In 1966 I testified before two Senate committees. I thought they were open—they weren't.

Indeed, during the Johnson administration, medical and scientific people—backed by the Kennedys—urged that drugs be administered by the Department of Health, Education and Welfare, while law-and-order people politicked for the Department of Justice. With the decision to turn drug control over to the police, LSD was made illegal, and most of the top drug scientists began their steady exit from government responsibility.

THE PUBLIC WAS OBSESSED

In the spring of 1966, public interest in LSD had reached a level of obsession. A cover story in *Life Magazine* had presented a fair—almost pro—picture of the promise of LSD. This was no accident. Henry Luce, founder of *Life* and *Time* magazines, had taken LSD himself and enjoyed it. While Luce lived, *Life's* treatment of LSD was always scientific and fair.

ASKED TO TESTIFY BEFORE THE SENATE

About this time I was approached by Carl Perian, staff director for a Senate committee on narcotics—a thoughtful, sophisticated man who had done considerable homework before coming to visit. He wanted me to testify before hearings of a Special Subcommittee of the Committee on the Judiciary United States Senate on LSD and Marihuana Use on College Campuses to be chaired by Senator Thomas J. Dodd of Connecticut.

After several meetings with Mr. Perian I agreed to testify, with the assurance that Senator Dodd would be respectful and not hostile.

5

MiLLBrOOK RaiDED

BY ROSEMary Leary

IN THE SPrING OF 1966, we planted an early garden
at Millbrook , reseeding the Heavenly Blue Morning Glories. Each weekend, the main house on the estate
was full of visitors. There were fifteen or so on this particular April night. My future husband Tim Leary, his son Jack
and I were in the bedroom on the third floor smoking mint
leaves and DMT when we heard a loud noise from below.
Jack went to investigate. He came back, slamming the door.
There were a bunch of hunters, men with guns down there.

Sounds of heavy booted feet echoed through the house,
up stairs. I shoved the glass pipe and the vial of DMT under
the covers. Suddenly, the beaded curtain between the dressing
room and the bedroom was pushed aside and at least ten men
burst into the room. I thought they look rather chest-fallen to
find a peaceful family scene instead of the orgy they'd surely
been anticipating. They led Tim and Jack downstairs and told
me not to move, so I stayed in bed. A nervous young state
trooper held a spotlight on me.

The light hurt my eyes, so I asked the trooper to move it away. As he turned, I checked the pipe with my toes. Then three frowning men with clipboards came in, hurriedly turned out the drawers and closets and called in a photographer to record the mess. A leather jacketed snooper trooper poked fingers into creams and lotions, sniffed at my cologne. Another looked under the bed. A third dropped old birth control pills into an envelope, licked the flap and said, *"You can getup and go down stairs with the others."*

G. GORDON LIDDY IN MY BEDROOM

The dining room was usually lit by candles. Floodlights gave it a detective-story look, highlighting the old wall tapestries to which we had added emerald fields and amber birds in day-glow paint. In the middle of this baronial atmosphere Sheriff Quinlan of Dutchess County interrogated the guest. Standing next to him was G. Gordon Liddy, formerly with the FBI and soon to be the local district attorney. He had been the first into our room, with a gun in his hand.

I recognized Liddy from his-clenched face newspaper photographs, when soon after our first arrest in Laredo, Texas, he'd promised the local newspapers he would "crack down hard on drugs." This raid was his bid for fame in Dutchess County New York. He whispered into the sheriff's ear.

I recognized Liddy from his clenched-face newspaper photographs.

Tim demanded that the phone be reconnected so he could call a lawyer. A deputy said that was the phone company's problem, not his. A trooper kept a gun trained on a peace loving Great Dane, who had been asleep next to his owner when their room was invaded. A berry invader tried to make friends with the children he had frightened awake.

A police matron led two outraged and crying women journalists into the room. They had planned to interview the residents for *Life Magazine*. The journalists were made to strip and their arms and legs examined for needle marks. The Sheriff asked another guest, a young woman, if she had had sexual intercourse that night.

It was almost dawn before Liddy and the Sheriff finished listing everyone and photographing everything and the housebreakers had made off with family photographs, books, bottles of wine and my favorite fuchsia plant. The Sheriff put a firm hand on Tim's shoulder and escorted him into a black police car while his minions guarded the rest of us. Then they too drove down the long, maple-shaded drive in an orderly cortege of black Fords and Pontiacs.

February 7, 2002
Rosemary
Woodruff joined
her husband
Timothy Leary on
the other side to
share strawberry
field's forever.

Bill Young - The San Francisco Chronicle

Rosemary and Timothy in 1969.

NTO THE NGHT

Downstairs, musicians were already composing songs about "The Raid". I changed out of my nightgown and set off in an old Studabaker to find a telephone. The only phone available was in an all-night diner near Poughkeepsie, but the diner was crowded with laughing, backslapping police officers eating apple pie.

I continued into town. Bloodhounds were baying in the kennel behind the red brick jailhouse; the man at the desk inside shouted above the clamor that he would tell me nothing. So I went beck to the diner—now nearly deserted—and called a defense fund lawyer in New York City. "*Millbrook was raided. They took Tim. No, I don't know how much bail will be,*" I reported.

> Tim thrived on being the Tragic Hero— the sweet dream of oppression.

"Control of Dangerous Drugs! Maintaining a Public Nuisance! Adultery!" the charges screamed out from the report. Nevertheless, Tim was released on bail later in the day. Good humored and unworried, he seemed to have enjoyed this new confrontation with the law. He appeared to thrive on the media response, the urgent need for fund and lawyers, the threat of a trial and prison sentence, the myth of the Tragic Hero, and the sweet dream of oppression.

At Liddy's instigation, a grand jury was convened to investigate the Castalia Foundation, with me as the star witness. I declined to answer their questions. Tim decided on a Hindu religious defense—which was as effective as a pagan defense would have been in Salem.

MaKING POLITICaL HISTOrY

"Don't you realize," Tim said, *"this will be the first court test of LSD. You'll be making legal, scientific, philosophical, political, and religious history! The case could go on for years! Beginning right here in Poughkeepsie, we could change the world! We'll get Allen Ginsberg and peyote roadmen to testify. We'll get Lama Govinda from India. We'll fill the courtroom with chanters, Tibetan gongs, flowers, incense . . . ."*

I faced a twenty-five day sentence for each unanswered question.

𝕻𝖔𝖚𝖌𝖍𝖐𝖊𝖊𝖕𝖘𝖎𝖊 𝕵𝖔𝖚𝖗𝖓𝖆𝖑
POUGHKEEPSIE, N.Y.
Feb 24 1967

MISS ROSEMARY WOODRUFF

Leary Aide Involved:

Appeals Court Agrees To Hear Woodruff Case

The Court of appeals, highest court in the state, has agreed to hear the case of Miss Rosemary Woodruff. She was convicted of contempt of curt for refusing to testify in an investigation of Dr. Timothy Leary.

Noel Tepper, Miss Woodruff's attorney, said today he was notified by telephone of the court's decision.

Miss Woodruff, administrative aide to Leary at his Castalia Foundation in Millbrook, spent 27 days in the Dutchess County Jail on the contempt charge. She had refused to testify before a grand jury on the grounds it would violate her religious beliefs.

Tepper contends her constitutional right to religious freedom was violated. The question, he said today, is between the right of an individual to remain silent and the right of the state to force a person to talk.

The district attorney's office maintains the appeal is academic since Miss Woodruff has served her sentence and the case has been closed.

Leary and three other associates were indicted on narcotics charges by the grand jury. The indictments were dismissed in September, however. District Attorney John Heilman Jr. said statements made by the defendants could not be used against them under new U. S. Supreme court rulings.

After Leary was imprisoned in 1970, Rosemary helped him breakout and the couple fled to Algeria to join up with the Black Panthers. When Leary was captured in 1973, Rosemary went underground where she lived under a variety of identities, in locations ranging from Afghanistan to Columbia to Cape Cod—until all warrants against her were dropped in 1994.

I spent a month in jail for contempt. The bloodhounds kept me awake for most of the night. Midway
through my sentence I was called by the matron into the
visitor's room. I thought I was going to be let go but she
pointed to the television screen where Ted Kennedy was
shaking his finger at Tim. Kennedy was making point for
his constituents, denouncing those who used drugs as
being deranged. Tim answered with the need for controls,
licenses and not a word about religion. He seemed rather
mad-professorish and clearly rattled by Kennedy's aggres-
sive manner.

Tim did better with Senator Dodd's inquiries, even
venturing to say "*Gawd*" in that unique Boston way. My
life had become strange, but watching Tim on television
while in jail was stranger than anything I'd ever experienced outside of LSD. With two days off for good behavior, I was released. I had two days to roam the woods
before I testified or went back to jail.

For the next thirty days, I appeared before the Grand
Jury. It was that or face a twenty-five day sentence for *each*
unanswered question. So I looked at their pictures of the
disorderly mansion and answered questions about my use
of drugs and why I used them. "*To increase and expand my
consciousness. To know the nature of God and the Universe,
Sir.*"

The charges were dropped. There were no indict-
ments against anyone. Tim and I moved into a teepee on
Ecstasy Hill on The Millbrook estate. For a very brief time
I was able to go back to the woods and gardens.

But soon enough, there were other raids and finally
the headlines in the local paper blared, "Religious Pres-
ence at Millbrook Ended". There was a photograph of a
bearded, Buddha-carrying community member being
escorted out of the estate gates by a state trooper.

6

TESTIFYING BEFORE THE SENATE

I WENT TO WASHINGTON accompanied by
my two children, Susan and Jack. My wife,
Rosemary, was in jail that month for refusing
to testify in front of a grand jury arranged in
Poughkeepsie, New York, by the local assistant
D.A.—none other than G. Gordon Liddy, who was to
be a central figure in the Watergate caper a few years
later.

There was enormous press coverage. The hallways
in front of the large hearing room were crowded with
television reporters. As I started to enter the chambers,
I was approached by Mr. Perlan, who looked a bit
harassed. It seemed that Senator Dodd's hearing was to
be upstaged by the unexpected arrival of another
committee member, Senator Edward Kennedy of Massachusetts. Teddy was scheduled to be out of town, but
hearing about the press coverage, he flew back to the
capital—much to the dismay of Mr. Perian and Senator
Dodd, and me.

I Read My Prepared Statement

As I took my place at the witness table, Senator Dodd smiled reassuringly. My eyes met Teddy's, and he looked away uneasily. You know the look.

I began reading my prepared statement. *"I am particularly grateful to come before this committee, because I think the most constructive legislation in this admittedly complex field has come from this committee. I am very aware of the work done by the chairman of the committee in constructive remedy to the narcotic drug problem . . . ."*

I continued to tell the committee that psychedelic drugs are nonaddictive, nontoxic, and antinarcotic. We don't know exactly what they do. They seem to release neurological energies. My position was that energy is not dangerous if used wisely. There is nothing to fear from our own nervous systems or from our own cellular structures.

On the basis of the statistics so far, I told the committee that I would say there is more violence, insanity, friction, terror in cocktail lounges and barrooms on any one Saturday night than in the entire 23-year history of LSD use. The so-called peril of LSD resides precisely in its eerie power to release ancient, wise, at times even holy sources of energy, inside the human brain.

WHY OUR BEST AND BRIGHTEST?

During the preceding months of heated pub-
licity and occasional bureaucratic hand-wring-
ing about LSD, one simple question had remained unanswered: Why were our most intelligent,
gifted, best-educated young people choosing to expose
themselves to this new and admittedly strange experience?

My answer, like the LSD experience itself, may
have been a stiff dose for those
unwilling to look at the record of
history. We have at hand energies
easily available, which are accepted
eagerly by the young and abhorred
by the older generation, and what
is worse, we have a communication
breakdown between the two generations. The challenge of the
psychedelic chemicals is not just
how to control them, but how to
use them. Restrictive legislation
which creates a new class of college
educated white-collar criminals is obviously not the
answer.

**The peril of LSD
resides in its
eerie power to
release ancient,
wise, at times
even holy
sources of
energy.**

Research, training, knowledge, are the only solutions to this problem. But here we reach the center of
the communication breakdown, because to the older
generation, "drug" means medicine, disease, doctor, or
dope fiends, addicts, crime. But to the vast majority of
young people experimenting with these new psychedelic chemicals, the word "drug" obviously means

positive things—possible growth, opening up the mind, beauty, sensual awareness, and in some cases, a religious revelation.

WIDE RANGE OF PSYCHOACTIVE CHEMICALS

The word "drug" covers a very wide range of psychoactive chemicals. On the one hand, the narcotic escape drugs—opiates, heroin, barbiturates, and alcohol—muffle consciousness and contract awareness. The psychedelic drugs—very different pharmacologically—seem to open up consciousness and accelerate awareness. The theories and laws necessary to control narcotics may not have any application to these other substances.

> **The challenge of psychedelics is not just how to control them, but how to use them.**

I was just getting into my stride. I reminded the committee that a previous witness said that LSD users were very eager to talk about their experiences. They weren't like junkies; they didn't feel like criminals . . .

7

SPECIAL LEGISLATION NEEDED

INTERRUPTING, and addressing me as Mr. Leary (Hmmmm . . .?) Senator Kennedy challenged my testimony. *"Mr. Leary, I am trying to follow the best I possibly can some themes that must be coming out of your testimony here this morning, and I am completely unable to do so. You talked in the beginning about the communications problem which exists between different generations, and then you indicate and describe why that exists. Then we hear a description and analysis, as valuable as that might be, about the different reactions to different drugs."*

"I am completely unable to follow anything other than just sort of a general hyperbole of discussion here. Since your testimony isn't written, and this is a matter with which we are deeply concerned, I hope at least for those of us who are not intimitably as familiar as apparently you are with LSD,

that you will try and see if you can analyze this somewhat more precisely. At least I would find that helpful. As I say, I haven't had the background or experience in this area as I am sure the other members of the committee have, but I think it would be extremely valuable if you could at least outline to some extent what you are going to try and demonstrate here today."

WHAT F I TURNED TEDDY ON?

As I listened to Teddy's incoherence I amused myself the notion of turning him on and wondered if it would help him get this thoughts together. *"I was, Senator Kennedy, just about to point out the differences that exist among drugs, and I am going to suggest that special types of legislation are needed."*

Cutting me off again, Kennedy demanded, *"Are you going to talk about the lack of communication between the generations before that or after that?"*

LICENSE USE

Duh? *"I finished doing that,"* I answered. Then returning to the salient point I explained that I felt constructive legislation was badly needed, and I recommended *respectfully* that the committee consider legislation which would license responsible adults to use these drugs for serious purposes. To obtain such a license, the applicant should have to meet physical, intellectual, and emotional criteria.

I told the committee that I believed that the criteria for marijuana, the mildest of the psychedelic drugs, should be similar those used to license people to drive automobiles, whereas the criteria for the licensing of much more powerful LSD should be much more strict—perhaps similar to the criteria used for airplane pilots would be appropriate.

Train Young People

I further urged the committee to make some provision for young people to be trained in the use of these powerful instruments. If a high percentage of college students were using these instruments, we could drive them underground, or we could legitimize their use in carefully controlled circumstances. At the end of the century, this question came to the fore again with medical marijuana. The voters wisely agreed with my premise that using the control of a doctor's prescription was smarter than driving people underground to obtain their medicine.

"Everyone says give LSD to the medical profession." I went on with my prepared testimony. *"The medical profession has had LSD for 23 years and hasn't known what to do with it, because LSD is not a medicine that cures physical problems. It is a psychological educational tool."*

HOW IS IT MANUFACTURED?

Senator Dodd cut in this time, asking, *"Can you tell us where it is manufactured?"*

I replied that the original patent holder of LSD was Sandoz Laboratories in Switzerland, although we were told it was made in Czechoslovakia and Mexico. I explained that LSD comes from the chemist in an extremely powerful powder. One gram of powder can produce between 10,000 and 20,000 doses. The powder is then usually diluted in some form of liquid, and then broken down and used in that form.

NORMAL DOSE

Pursuing the details, Dodd asked what I considered to be a normal dose and I answered that it depends on your purpose. If you want to have a deep, out-of-the-mind experience, you would probably take 300 gamma. LSD, of course, has a tremendous range. A small amount of LSD is like marijuana. A large amount of LSD is a full-fledged, 12-hour, out-of-the mind experience. There is no known lethal dose, but one danger of black-market LSD is you are never sure what you are getting so that when LSD is put on sugar cubes, you never know whether you are getting 100 gamma or 300 gamma. This accounts for some of the problems in indiscriminate black-market use.

Next Dodd wanted to know if I had used it myself, which seemed a little off, since it was widely publicized that I had. Remember, at the time of this Senate hearing use of LSD was not yet criminalized. Being ever forthright, I acknowledged that I had used LSD or similar drugs 311 times in the previous 6 years. Each time I took LSD I kept careful records and I had a specific purpose in mind why I was doing it—the way a scientist would look at different objects through his magnifying lens. I told the committee that I had, under my personal supervision, witnessed over 3,000 ingestions of LSD.

LSD EFFECTS

Dodd wondered if I could "briefly" describe its effect? *"No Sir. Each segment of an LSD experience is very complicated."* I answered and then explained that thousands of memory cards or thousands of sensory molecules are firing off. There is no amnesia. You remember all of this, so it would take 20 hours to describe an LSD experience.

LSD's hallucinations are experiences for which we don't have words.

"One example, sir, would perhaps point up some of the paradoxes," I continued. I described how a psychiatrist might read about sexual abnormalities and hallucinations and then one day into his office walks a person who describes an LSD experience. He might say: *"I was sitting there and suddenly I began to dissolve. Every cell in*

my body began to break down, and I was afraid I would become a puddle on the floor. Then I saw a huge serpent swallow me. I went in the serpent's stomach. Later I was excreted and I exploded. Then I became an animal. I could feel hair and claws growing on my body. Then I could look down and see fishy scales as though I were a reptile. Then I was floating as though I was a single-celled organism."

By this time, even the most experienced psychiatrist is likely to be crouching under the table, saying, *"In 30 years of my practice I have never listened to anything so frightening and so far out."* On the other hand, Hindu would say, *"Oh, yes; the third dream of Vishnu."*

Neurological Basis

I explained that we also have neurological and anatomical explanations for LSD's so-called hallucinations. They are not supernatural; they are experiences for which we don't have words. I said that I expected future research would allow us to understand, control, and even produce hallucinations that won't be mysterious or frightening.

Dodd said that the committee had heard about people jumping out of windows and eating bark off trees and grass off of lawns and committing crimes as a result of the use.

I acknowledged that in some cases, when LSD is used by people who are not trained, under very poor circumstances, bizarre behavior develops. As more people are trained in how to use this, and as they know where to use this drug, these episodes will be cut down.

AND VIOLANCE?

Law enforcement officers and the psychiatric clinics
saw that one case in 1,000 who is having trouble. I was
getting about 100 letters a week from people who rhapsodize
about the positive aspects, so it seemed at times we were talking
about two entirely different experiences. There is no evidence
then—or now—that any case has resulted in homicide. In fact,
years later Art Linkletter recanted the highly publicized story
that his daughter had jumped from a window to her death while
under the influence of LSD.

Unconvinced Dodd said there was evidence before the
committee regarding such cases. *"Weren't you here this morning
when Captain Trembly told about the youngster who tried to kill her
mother after using LSD?"* he challenged. He went on to point to
Dr. Louria who had told the committee the day before about
the homicidal tendencies of users, their destructive conduct
with respect to their physical surroundings. *"Doesn't this make it
perfectly clear that the use of it brings on such activities?"*

I agreed that these things may have occurred. However, of
all the forms of energy available to the American citizen, I
assured the committee that LSD was statistically producing
fewer cases of violence or destruction than alcohol or some of
our more popular medications.

Dodd was unconvinced. *"You don't offer that as a very good
argument—it just doesn't do as much damage as something else."*

Continuing with my effort to bring reason and balance to
the hearing I said that the problem for me was that this one
case of LSD panic got headlines, whereas 999 cases of LSD
revelation nobody cared about. So to be scientific about this,
we would have to have some batting average. In any 1,000
people, one is likely to become violent within the next 6
months. Naturally, if he takes LSD, it may still happen and
would have happened without the LSD.

8

THEY IGNORED COMMON GROUND

SOUNDING LIKE a PrOSECUTOR, Dodd pursued his point. *"Would you agree that uncontrolled use is dangerous? Don't you feel that LSD should be put under some control, or restriction as to its sale, its possession, and its use?"*

"Definitely!" I emphatically agreed. In the first place, I said that I thought that the 1965 Drug Control Act, which the committee sponsored, was the high watermark in such legislation. But I was urging some form of licensing, or we will have another era of prohibition in this country, because the people who were using LSD were not criminal types. They were middle-class college people who were very aware of their constitutional rights to change their consciousness as long as they are not visibly harming society.

> Tim looked rather mad-professorish and clearly rattled.
> —*Rosemary Leary*

Ted Kennedy jumped in, saying that the *New Republic* article says right in there rather clearly stated, *"It is more likely that the individuals who use this are usually already psychiatrically deranged before taking LSD. This, of course, emphasizes even more the absolute necessity of competent psychiatric screening of every person who is to use any kind of hallucinogens. "*

Again I emphasized that I agreed with that conclusion. I restated that I was urging that there be some kind of licensing.

Ignoring our common ground, Kennedy continued his attack. *"I thought the point made by the chairman about the types of people who are using it substantiates not only what the chairman observed but it was also previously testified so, and so I think there has been substantial evidence to that matter, that those that do use it are already psychologically deranged or can be, or at least the predominance that are using it lean that way. At least that is the testimony which has been presented to this committee. Now if you have different conclusions on that, I think that from either your years of study or others, I think it would be helpful to have that material."*

I HAD TO DISAGREE

I could not allow Stanford students to be described as psychotic or criminal. In his *New Republic* article Dr. O'Chota said, *"A sample of students at Stanford University showed that at least 40 percent have been taking hallucinogens."* I was willing to defend very fiercely the sanity and the social constructiveness of the 40 percent of the Stanford University student body, even though I may be unpopular

Brushing my defense aside, Kennedy persisted. *"That is not responsive to the question, but I will accept the statement. Mr. Leary, I have been continually confused by your testimony. Maybe that is my own limitation of understanding as to the nature of the subject that we are considering here today. You mentioned earlier, and I am trying to clarify at least to some extent my own understanding, that you needed a microscope in order to indicate the degree or quantity in which this LSD should be taken. Is that correct?"*

KENNEDY MaDE UP HIS MIND

Is he being deliberately obtuse? I wondered. Or perhaps he has been enjoying *his* drugs of choice a little too frequently. *"As a metaphor, yes, Sir,"* I clarified.

Continuing with his pointless thrust, Kennedy demanded, *"And do you use it to measure the quantity, to make up the consistency of the particular drug at a particular time to determine what kind of ride you want to have? Is that right?"*

"I am using the microscope as a metaphor, Sir." I repeated, trying to get Kennedy on to the same page. But Kennedy persisted with his demands, *"And then they take these—you say that they get 25 grains?"* "Gamma." I corrected. *"Pardon?"* Kennedy asked insistently. *"Gamma, that is 25 millionths of a gram,"* I explained.

"Twenty-five gamma, and then they get 300 to go out of their minds by virtue of its use?" Kennedy asked rhetorically. He had obviously made up his mind on the issue.

BeTraYeD!

"Yes, sir." I demurred. As I listened to Teddy's attempt to bluster and bully, I was stunned in disbelief. What a disloyal snake! My family had known and supported young Jack when he was a stripling congressman from Boston. I had talked at length with Jack and was well aware of both his and Bobby's

> **I never urged anyone to take LSD. I deplore indiscriminate use.**

intelligent—hedonic use of drugs. Dr. Jack, the "White House medicine man", was my friend. And here was Teddy, of all people, pushing Carl Perian and Thomas Dodd aside to gain respectability points by lynching me!

My attention snapped back to Kennedy. *"Now, when they go out of their minds, as I gather from your testimony that they certainly can, if they go out of their minds—let's just say if they go out of their minds, do they know the difference between right and wrong?"*

"No, Sir," I responded. *"Not social right and wrong. They are likely to think in an unconventional—"*

Cutting me off, Kennedy completed my sentence. *"In unconventional ways. And so if they don't really know the difference between right and wrong, still they are able to, as you say, perform normal kinds of activities, bodily or social activities?"*

Training Is Essential

Hoping to get back to my agenda I answered that that depended entirely on the experience of the person. You see you have to be trained to use LSD the way you are trained to use a computer. An unprepared person is confused.

Kennedy asked if I were suggesting that anyone who is going to administer LSD ought to be highly trained. *"Absolutely!"* I affirmed.

Pursuing the point like a bird dog on a scent, Kennedy pressed on. *"And that there shouldn't be indiscriminate use? And that is why you want to give college courses in LSD? And what is going to happen to the boy who doesn't get to college?"* I explained that there would be special training institutes for him.

"So we are going to train high school students as well?" Kennedy demanded sarcastically. Sensing a trap, I emphasized that I would let research, scientific research, answer the question as to what age the nervous system is ready to use these new instruments.

"That is very responsive," Kennedy snorted. *"Now you feel that anybody who distributes this ought to be carefully trained, is that correct? Where are they going to get this preparation?"*

PSYCHEDELIC TRAINING CAMPS

Ignoring the contempt, I explained that for the previous 5 years, my training institute, the Castalia Foundation, had been the only one in the world that has been conscientiously and systematically training people.

Unrelenting, Kennedy persisted. He pointed out that other people, who hadn't had the good opportunity or fortune to attend our institute, were taking LSD and asked in his rhetorical way if the committee oughtn't "to at least be conscious of the dangers" presented by LSD use until the Castalia Foundation could expand its training.

I emphatically repeated what I'd already said. The need for licensing legislation was desperate. We had to get institutes trained and licensed so that people could receive training. Again, I reminded them of our common ground—the 1965 Drug Control Act, with which I agreed completely.

Cutting me off, Senator Dodd asked if I were suggesting that the federal government and the state governments ought to control the training. "Exactly!" I agreed. I repeated yet again that I was in 100 percent agreement with the 1965 Drug Control Act and I wished the states would follow the wisdom of the committee and follow with exactly that kind of legislation.

Bursting in, Kennedy demanded to know if I agreed that there should not be indiscriminate distribution of LSD. *"I have never suggested that, Sir!"* On the defensive I insisted that I had never urged anyone to take LSD. I have always deplored indiscriminate or unprepared use.

No Penalty
For Possession

"And there ought to be strict regulations then with regards to those who possess it?" Kennedy continued in his prosecurorial fashion. *"No, Sir."* I quickly answered. This was something I felt strong about. College kids should not be into criminals.

"Well, now wait a moment, Dr. Leary." Kennedy's eyes met mine. *"You just stated somewhat earlier that you thought anybody who was going to use it ought to be carefully trained, ought to understand. I don't find the consistency of your argument when you say that we ought to have careful restrictions on LSD, strict control over its production, but that we shouldn't have strict control over who has it. How do you—"*

Impatiently, I interrupted Teddy. *"Because I urge all of us to face reality."* I described the way in which millions of Americans are using this drug indiscriminately in their own pursuits. Emphatically, I explained that I was not in favor of passing laws, which would put 40 percent of the Stanford University student body in the category of criminals. *"I am against laws which would put such people in prison."*

> I opposed passing laws that would call 40 percent of the Stanford University student body criminals.

Let Research Rule

Ignoring this important point, Dodd asked if the research with respect to LSD is still going on. I explained that while some research continued most had been almost halted because of the present hysteria. There were very few government-approved grants because of the grand panic that was sweeping the country. Doctors and psychiatrists who should have been doing studies were afraid to.

I assured the committee that if research showed any serious physiological side effects, or irreversible psychological effects, I would be the first one to urge LSD's ban. I was sincere. Having taken LSD perhaps more than any scientist in the world, I was more curious than anyone as to its physiological effect or possibilities of brain damage. Every time I met someone who asked about contraindications, I would say, *"Will you please wire me collect if you have any personal information on brain damage?"*

But Is LSD Dangerous?

Brushing aside all that I had just said, Kennedy returned to the *New republic* article in which I'd been quoted and asked I I'd noted that the author said, *"There is one uniform agreement among the investigators of LSD, namely, that LSD can be extremely dangerous when used improperly."*?

I was getting impatient with the *New Republic* article being held up as the ultimate authority. *"Sir, the motor car is dangerous if used improperly. I couldn't be in more agreement,"* I quipped.

Seeming oblivious to my sarcasm, Kennedy pressed the point. *"It is dangerous, then?"* *"If used improperly,"* I clarified. *"Isn't that why the pilot is licensed as well?"* Kennedy continued. *"Yes, Sir,"* I answered impatiently. *"Human stupidity and ignorance is the only danger human beings face in this world."*

Teddy Twisted My Words

Apparently satisfied that he'd heard enough, Kennedy said, *"It seems to me that your testimony has been extremely convincing about the dangers of this drug, as well as its opportunities. And I think for someone who has been associated as long as you have been, have been intimately involved in it as long as you have been, I think that is extremely weighty evidence which you have given to this committee this morning, and we want to thank you."*

"I cannot agree with that summary." I protested. *"Respectfully. I must disagree, Senator Kennedy, with your statement."*

"Let's take the various aspects of it. You feel that there ought to be control over at least importation? The sale and manufacturing?" Kennedy said with the air of a man having made up his mind. *"Yes, Sir,"* I agreed."

"And that the only reason you think this is because it is a matter of interstate and foreign commerce? Is that the only reason? I mean, we have things which are produced, textiles in Massachusetts, furniture in Massachusetts that are not restricted, Dr. Leary..."

Sitting there watching Teddy huff and puff in law-school rhetorical style, hidden behind the robes of legislative cliche, I felt sorry for Teddy—and for the rest of us.

9

BOBBY'S TRAP

AFTER THE HEARING, I was invited to lunch by a group of young men and women who worked on the staffs of five senators. They had all taken LSD and were much concerned about the Kennedys' attempts to abuse psychedelic drugs. Ironically enough, one of these young men was from Bobby's staff.

In those days one could be more open about one's own "experiments." After a jolly hour of psychedelic reminiscing, they got down to business. It seemed that Bobby was going to hold hearings on LSD too, and was planning to invite me as the first witness—and this had them worried.

It would be foolish to venture onto Bobby's turf.

"Just because Teddy's bumbling made it easy for you, don't be fooled. Bobby is another story. Ask anyone around Washington, and they will tell you that Bobby is the most ruthless, efficient, brilliant investigator on the hill. He'll have mountains of

*staff work. He'll be ready. For example, he'll produce
records from Sandoz Laboratories, showing that you never
received a microgram of acid from them. Do you realize
what that means?"*

"Yes," I replied. *"He'll try to make it look as though all
our research has been illegal." "You got it,"* said my infor-
mant. *"Bobby is also working closely with Dr. Sidney
Cohen, who is coaching the senator on ways to trip you up.
Naturally, we'd like to see you blast through the hearings
and teach these dinosaurs something about what's happening
with young people. But we cannot overemphasize the
danger. Bobby is bright and tough."*

TESTFY or PLay IT SaFe?

In the following days we were kept very busy
with local political harassment. We snatched up
Rosemary from the Poughkeepsie County Court
House and hid out in the woods to escape the minions
of Gordon Liddy.

Coordinating the Leary Defense Committee, public
lectures, dictating the *Playboy* interview. I was still
undecided about whether to tangle with Bobby. The
day before the hearings, we held a strategy meeting
lying panoramically on the blue-copper roof of the 64-
room mansion in Millbrook. We decided that it would
be foolish to venture onto Bobby's turf in a situation
where he controlled all the levers. Reckless to be cross-
examined without the protections of counsel. A no-win
setup.

So I Prepared a Statement

My prepared statement would be hand-delivered by one of our top operatives, Larry Bogart, a pioneer conservationist-ecologist. A most respectable and straight person, not a doper, Larry had been horrified by my 30-year marijuana sentence at Laredo, Texas, and was managing the Leary defense. Larry looked like a pink-cheeked, Princeton professor of Ancient Languages.

So it happened on May 24, 1966. Bobby opened his hearings before the Subcommittee on Executive Reorganization of the Committee on Government Operations. The television cameras whirred and my name was called, up walked Larry Bogart to read the Statement of Timothy Leary, Ph.D., President, Castalla Foundation for Psychedelic Research, Millbrook, N.Y.

The statement began by pointing to increasing numbers of Americans who were taking LSD, despite laws banning its use. A high proportion of users were young-college and high school students. Since new state and federal legislation had closed off legitimate access to LSD, almost all supplies were coming from illicit sources. This state of affairs made several million otherwise law-abiding American citizens into criminals; fostered the growth of black market profiteering; increased the likelihood of impure and contaminated LSD, with unpredictable effects; blocked research into a scientific tool of enormous potential; and tended to undermine public faith in the law.

Prior to that time, fully half of the nation's hospital beds had been occupied by mental patients. The discovery of a host of increasingly effective synthetic organic chemicals had dramatically cut hospital stays. Mind-relaxing drugs and tranquilizers had restored millions to useful lives in society. But emotional problems are still with us, and it seemed the best investment we could make lay in further research in molecular biology.

The statement pointed to an international confer-ence held in May of 1965 in Amityville, N.Y. where psychiatrists and psychologists reported on the use of LSD to treat the mentally ill. Dr. Harold Abramson, a brilliant pioneer researcher who served as host and sponsor of the confer-ence, was prevented by govern-ment policy at the time from pursuing his investigations. The only way out of the situation was a

We need a program for using these psychedelic gifts wisely.

cooling-off period, while rational examination was conducted by scientists with government officials. I had volunteered as an evidence of cooperation to forego the use of any psychedelic material presently held illegal, and have urged others to do likewise.

PSYCHOCHEMICAL COMMISSION NEEDED

I suggested a Commission of Psychochemical Education—a blue-ribbon panel of neurologists, pharmacologists, psychologists, educators, and religious leaders to survey the entire field of psy-chochemical research, to evaluate the educational uses of LSD, "learning pills," RNA stimulators, and to anticipate the social and psychological effects of new drugs which can expand and speed up the mind.

I urged the commission to propose a program for using these chemical gifts wisely. I suggest that for a year, there should be intensive research directed to ascertaining what risks, if any, attend the use of LSD and that the value of supportive setting and length of preparation should be accurately measured.

I Made a Call For Licensing

I suggested that a licensing procedure be set up, under the commission's guidance, to enable responsible, healthy adults to use LSD to further self-understanding. Persons with organic or psychological disability would be screened out, as would potential schizophrenics. Licenses would be given only to persons who had undergone adequate training by experienced LSD guides. Should the user prove irresponsible, he would lose his license and be penalized for breaking the law, just as anyone else. The establishment of special licensing procedures for a new class of chemicals has a precedent in the case of radioisotopes, which are controlled by the AEC (Atomic Energy Commission).

That this could work was demonstrated years later when cities set up a kind of licensing of users in response to the medical marijuana laws which were overwhelmingly approved by the voters at the end of the 20th Century. People with legitimate medical conditions were given prescriptions—which were reviewed annually by their physicians—and "cannabis buyers clubs" were established in dozens of cities where suffers could purchase medical grade cannabis. The government huffed and puffed. Peter McWilliams, author of some ten self-help books and aids victim, was Federally prosecuted and convicted. Denied his medicine he choked to death on his vomit—even though cannabis has been proven effective in quelling nausea. Nonetheless, the sky did not fall in. Marijuana users were able to legally obtain pot to soothe their pains. Licensing was effective. Once again demonstrating that "we the people" are smarter than our politicians who create the laws to which we must submit.

> **The right to change your consciousness using drugs was a basic tenet of the counter-culture.**

In my statement before the subcommittee I proposed that LSD be administered only in special Psychedelic Training Centers, where a team of experienced guides would be available to screen, prepare, and guide applicants. Medical supervision would be provided and FDA surveillance exercised. LSD, available at relatively low cost in such centers, would reduce the demand for black market supplies, and the attendant undesirable consequences previously mentioned. LSD accidents would be minimized and, should they occur, would be handled by experienced staff.

Bobby was furious at my wariness about his ambush, but he got over it and we became friends again.

10

I was Free!

ON DECEMBER 12, 1968, the appeal was argued before the Supreme Court. On May 19, 1969, a sunny day, the Federal marijuana prohibition was repealed. I was free!

My freedom was short lived, however. The Nixon administration moved to refile charges on the transportation technicality and I was, much to my chagrin, pulled back to Laredo to face the same judge and the same Federal agents. The judge sentenced me to ten years. Appeal bond is routinely granted in cases that do not involve violence, but not in my case. The judge denied bail on the grounds that the defendant was "going around the country preach-

> The defendant is going around the country preaching and teaching dangerous doctrines — Bail Denied!

ing and teaching dangerous doctrines." I was being persecuted—ah, prosecuted—for my beliefs and for writing about them.

POLITICAL OBSESSION

By 1968, debate over the Brain Change Option had become a political obsession. Every politician in the land was campaigning to stop the drug epidemic. For those who wished to change their brains, there was no more reliance on the religious metaphor or the First Amendment protections. The old Texas judges weren't buying that. The issue was now one of partisan politics. Forty million grass smokers and 7 million acid users were no longer content to appeal, like reservation Indians, to the Great White Father in Washington for peyote privileges. The right to change your consciousness using drugs had become a basic tenet of the counter-culture—along with the fight against racism and the war.

11

POLITICS OF ECSTASY

VERY SHORTLY AFTER we started our research in the 1960s, people began calling us a cult—a small group of people dedicated to an ideal. We pleaded guilty. We were a small group dedicated to an ideal.

> People called us a cult—a small group of people dedicated to an ideal.

Less than a decade later we were no longer a cult. According to a United Nations report in 1951, 200 million people had used marijuana and other cannabis-plant products. At that time in the United States, several million shared these values and methods—90% of them come from the young, racial or national minorities, or the creative.

Over 50,000,000 Americans have used marijuana, peyote, mescaline, and there are followers of other chemical yogas. Many millions of Americans rely upon tranquilizers to guide them through each day. Millions use energizers and pep pills. Close to 100 million Americans use alcohol, and are addicted to nicotine. Perhaps 100,000 people escape the turmoil and pain of life with heroin.

Our racial minorities, particularly Chicanos and blacks, use psychedelic drugs in much higher per-centage than the middle-class whites who pass most of our laws. The creative minority—poets, writers, musicians, dramatists, who use psychedelic drugs in a much higher percentage than other groups—are persecuted by the middle-aged, middle-class, middle-brows who pass our laws. The only way to deal with the psychochemical age is training. These drugs are going to be used. Ethical understand-ing will determine whether they are used to free or to imprison man's mind.

In dealing with psychochemicals, the only things we have to fear are ancient enemies—ignorance and panic.

As we moved into the psychochemical age, things got out of control. None of us knows exactly what the future will bring. But one thing's certain: psychochemicals release energy. In dealing with psychochemicals, the only things we have to fear are ancient enemies—ignorance and panic. The solution to the problems posed by psychochemicals is not imprisonment, its disciplined pursuit of knowledge.

The first problem is to know something about the different levels of consciousness. Unless you have some model or language for describing different states of brain function, you're operating in a state of confusion.

We Need a Language of Inner Space

In the past, men fought over symbols—the cross or the crescent, or which version of the Bible you used. In the 1960s and 70s the issue was which chemicals were part of your life and your growth.

The analogy I use is drawn from the science of optics. Three hundred years ago, if I announced there was a level of reality made up of tiny particles which seem to have a beauty, a meaning, a planfulness of their own, I'd be in danger of being imprisoned. When I could persuade people to look through the microscope lens at a leaf, or a snowflake, or a drop of blood, then they would discover that beyond the macroscopic world are visible realms of energy and meaning.

You learn how to get high.

But if I clapped a microscope onto your eye 300 years ago and said, "Walk around like this," you might trip over things. You might be entranced by the beauty of what you saw, but you would end up quite confused: "Well it's rather crazy and meaningless. I couldn't see anything I recognized."

The use of the microscope required that certain men spend hours peering through lenses at different forms of biological energy and—very slowly and painstakingly—develop a language. I could write a handbook explaining the different sorts of things you could see when you looked at a cross section of a plant. And then

you could look through the microscope and check out
my accuracy.

Similarly, there are levels of consciousness, defined
by the anatomical structures within the brain for decod-
ing energy. And each level of consciousness is inevitably produced by biochemical means, either by natural
biochemical events or by introduced chemicals that
move you to these different levels just as accurately as
the magnification of a lens moves you to different levels
of external reality.

The problem is, if the unprepared person takes LSD,
it's like plopping a microscope onto a man 300 years
ago. The prepared and knowledgeable use of marijuana
requires a complex yoga of attending to which stimuli
you are going to expose yourself to; which lenses you
are going to polish; which sense organs you are going to
open up; a very careful arrangement of the sequence
between external energy and a specific sense organ.
Like the microscope, using marijuana requires training,
practice, and a certain empirical mapping or language.

MIND EXPANSION IS NOT FOR EVERYONE

Expanding your vision, whether via the microscope or psychedelic drugs, is no business for
the neurotic person to get involved in. If you're
having trouble with simply being yourself and making a
living in this world, stay away from any experience that
is going to expand and multiply the complexities,
dimensions, and perspectives. You're simply going to
carry your confusion and your neurosis with you. If
you're not ready to look at yourself and your symbolic

aim, ambition, lusts, desires, pride, and complete self-ishness through a clear amplifying lens—stay away from any psychedelic experiences.

People often asked me how often, if ever, you should take LSD. Those of us who worked on our research project *never* said that anyone should take a psychedelic drug. The energy and power involved in changing your nervous system are too much.

BUT DOES LSD CAUSE PSYCHOSIS?

Psychosis is a sudden, unprepared-for confrontation with levels of energy that bewilder and terrorize you. A psychotic person, or a person having a prolonged LSD state, is suffering from a level of consciousness first reported by Buddha over 2,000 years ago. If you treat a psychotic as though he were looking at you with 2 billion years of neurological perspective, I think you would find yourself able to understand and be understood by him.

> The Buddha, after all, was one of the first dropouts.

THE RISK IS MINIMAL

Less than one in 1,000 people who take LSD have a prolonged severe negative reaction. Scientific evidence demonstrates that the danger of LSD is much less than the danger from using alcohol, nicotine, or even from jogging. But the awe that comes when the veil is torn from your eyes, and you see the nature of the energy process you're involved in, can be a most painful experience.

THE EXPERIENCE IS UNIVERSAL

Almost every visionary mystic in world history, such as Rama Krishna, Mohammed and even the founder of experimental psychology, Gustav Theodore Fechner—reported the same experience. Some sort of veil or symbolic reality was removed, and they stood there in trance, bewildered by the play of energy, searching for meaning deeper than the symbolic.

I'm concerned about anyone having one second of unexplained terror;

> What kind of a society will we have if we deprive young people of the right to aimless exploration, wandering, curious poking around, unskillful experiments in new forms of communication?

but I'm not concerned about a lot of young people taking a year or two to examine what this whole business is all about. What kind of a society will we have if we deprive young people of the right to aimless exploration, wandering, curious poking around, unskillful experiments in new forms of communication? The Buddha, after all, was one of the first dropouts.

New
Commandments

The problems posed by new ways of changing consciousness require two new commandments:

First Commandment: Thou shalt not alter the consciousness of thy fellow man by electrical or chemical means.

Can you change a man's consciousness if he wants you to? Can you teach him how? Yes, but the control of the method has got to be given to the man who owns that brain.

Second Commandment: Thou shalt not prevent thy fellow man from changing his consciousness by electrical or chemical means.

If someone's changing his consciousness wreaks clear harm to society, only then can you prevent him. In every such case, the burden of proof must be on society to demonstrate that harm is being done.

Awareness Brings an Existential Loneliness

A second reaction to the collapse of authority is existential loneliness. Once you have accepted that your nervous system creates your own reality from the Heraclitan flow, what guideposts, what compass readings, what new goals? This philosophic vacuum was temporarily filled by a renaissance of pessimistic, nostalgic creeds experiential Christianity, homogenized Buddhism, TV Hinduism—which served to shallow out, calm down the explosive expansions of the sixties.

NEW PHILOSOPHY OF SCIENTIFIC PAGANISM

I believe that a new philosophy created by those born after Hiroshima will:

1. Be scientific in essence and science-fiction in style;

2. Be based on the expansion of consciousness control of the nervous system, intellectual efficiency, and emotional equilibrium;

3. Stress individualism, decentralization of authority, live-and-let-live tolerance of difference, and a mind-your-own-business libertarianism;

4. Continue the trend toward open sexual expression and a more honest, realistic acceptance of the quality of and magnetic difference between the sexes;

5. Seek revelation and Higher Intelligence within natural processes, the nervous system, the genetic code, and in attempts to effect extraplanetary migration;

6. Assume physical immortality provided by scientists and encouraged by those intelligent enough to strive to live forever;

7. Be hedonic, esthetic, fearless, optimistic, loving.

12

Leary for Governor

IT WaS 1969. The more we thought about it, the better the idea it seemed—to run for governor of California. It promised to be great theatre, flamboyant fun, a bully platform from which to suggest change in the farce of partisan politics. And, as it turned out, there was some chance I might win.

The first step was newspaper endorsements. In a week we signed up *Rolling Stone, Berkeley Barb, Los Angeles Free Press, San Francisco Oracle, The San Diego Something-Or-Other*—in short, every underground paper in the state. The college dailies were delighted. Add 'em all up, and I had more circulation support than any of the other Democratic candidates. My platform statement was published in several California papers and stimulated the expected amused reactions.

> **There was some chance I would win.**

STATEWIDE 'PARTY'

The idea was to make the campaign a statewide party. The top rock 'n' roll and jazz groups in the world were willing to come help out. John Lennon wrote a campaign song based on the campaign motto: *"Come Together, Join the Party."* We planned to rent a railroad car and travel around the state with the greatest musicians and counterculture heroes—having enormous rallies in every city and town.

The demographics and statistical projections were interesting. I was running on the Democratic ticket against three other candidates—who neatly split the ticket. There was a right-winger: Mayor Sam Yorty of Los Angeles; a middle-of-the roader: Mayor Joseph Alioto of San Francisco, who pulled the old-line union vote; and a Kennedy man, Jesse Unruh, speaker of the state assembly.

> We would rent a railroad car and travel around the state with the greatest musicians and counterculture heroes.

My statisticians and poll experts estimated that I could win 33% of the Democratic vote—including young people, especially since the voting age had been dropped to 18, the astrology vote, the vegetarian vote, a lot of amused and sympathetic minority votes, the UFO vote, the kooks, the utopians, the dopers—hell, this was California we were talking about!

"Even if you don't beat Reagan in the general election," my advisors said, *"you'll end up titular leader of the Democratic party in California, and you'll change the texture of American politics forever."*

FUTIQUE NEWSCASTS

When the English movie crew arrived, the
campaign took on the media dimension necessary to win. The filmmakers wanted to do a
straight documentary—filming what happened. Past
participle. I said, *"No way!"*

We would film some rallies, some mass meetings,
but the main thrust of the film was to be futique newscasts, announcers reporting on the campaign. Initial
surveys would show the 15% kook vote going to me,
but then, as the film progressed and the rock concerts
and man-in-the-street interviews continued on film,
the fabricated newscasts would show my percentage
rising, rising.

Then the quotes from Nixon, Reagan, Agnew,
Premier Brezhnev, J. Edgar Hoover—taken from edited
news clips. of course—reacting, nervous about my
growing percentages. Last-minute help from the Beatles
and Jimi Hendrix, real endorsements from the children
of almost every major politician and media celebrity,
the final election night suspense, and then the victori-
ous campaign headquarter celebrations and shots—
dubbed—of my rivals conceding. The movie was to be
shot in January-February of 1970, edited in March, and
shown only in California the month before the June
primaries.

13

WHaT KIND OF a ParTY DO YOU WANT?

Now in the 21st Century, psychedelic brain change continues to be persecuted as Attorney Richard Glen Boire explains in his article on cognitive liberty at the end of this chronicle. Again, times are troubling and authoritarian government policies—supposedly required to protect us from terrorism—are threatening our freedoms. My campaign platform still sounds good and may be needed even more today.

Current political parties are no fun at all.

The purpose of government is to provide a joyous and harmonious pooling of intelligence to encourage a healthy life, individual liberty, and the pursuit of happiness for all citizens.

Ours was an Utopian Platform

Current political parties are no fun at all. They are grim and divisive organizations apparently committed to an unhealthy ecology, an uptight economy, centralized control, and violent tension among all citizens. Only a tiny minority really like the present miserable political system.

Affectionate Rewards

The present government penalizes the virtuous and rewards the immoral. Convicted felons are comfortably housed, doctored, well-fed, and allowed to loaf for years in the company of more skillful and glamorous outlaws who are delighted to teach them what they know. The sober, industrious, honest person is penalized by taxes, which support these maximum-security colleges of crime.

Prisons will be emptied of all but a few compulsively hung-up neurotics.

At present the only alternatives to violent authoritarianism is to start a New Party, based on a positive psychology of affectionate reward. This should be a rational, good-humored social system that rewards healthy, honest, harmoniously individualistic behavior and imposes gentle, appropriate, effective, constructive penalties upon unhealthy, dishonest, disharmonious behaviors.

PENALIZE
ASOCIAL BEHAVIOR

Clearly as a society we should reduce asocial behavior and increase positive, prolife behavior. Very different needs motivate three types of asocial behaviors, now defined as criminal.

CRIMES OF
VIOLENCE

The major function of the state is to protect the safety of its citizens. Persons convicted of violent crimes must be isolated in therapeutic reformatories, of varying degrees of security, until cured.

Actually, modern pharmacology knows enough right now to dramatically reduce the rate of violence on the basis of voluntary treatment. The possibilities of psychopharmacological rehabilitation of violent criminals was demonstrated at Concord in the Massachusetts State Prison back in 1961-64. Our focus should not be on punishment but on the conversion of incorrigibly violent prison convicts into wise, smiling productive citizens.

Violent behavior is caused by biochemical changes in the body that make the person feel bad. We demonstrated over and over how to neutralize violent emotions—help the person feel good in the context of a socially constructive, humane atmosphere. All voluntary, of course.

FINANCIAL RIP OFFS

Financial dishonesty should be penalized in the appropriate manner—financially. The way to reform an irrationally greedy thief is not to give an all-expense-paid refresher course in prison or to cage him like a violent person. The convicted larcenist should be allowed to work off his "score," forced to labor at union wages until he earns twice what he has stolen.

The victim can thus be given his money back. He's happy. The alert arresting officer gets a 25% bounty. He's happy. The remaining 25% goes to a state fund to repay larceny victims in cases where the crook fails to repay. When "something-for-nothing" dishonesty no longer pays, the crime rate will drop. The prisons will be emptied of all but a few compulsively hung-up neurotics who will be offered psychopharmacological relief.

These are admittedly emergency measures. In the harmonious hedonic society of the future any "crime" or "sinfulness" will automatically punish itself. It is the intrinsic nature of any "crime" that it inevitably carries its own penalty. The whiskey drinker has hangovers. The prostitute is cut off from sexual release. The gambler ends up broke. The smog producer has to live in smog. The hunter kills the creatures he was meant to learn from.

IMMORALITY

Immoral behaviors have always been a major source of political friction. A survey of history will show that every human behavior, from cheek-to-cheek dancing to female child murder, has been considered a capital crime in one culture and a holy sacramental act in another. Despite their irrational variance, however, moral codes are absolutely necessary for social survival. Morals and taboos are the very essence and "soul" of a society. The state has the obligation to administer the currently accepted moral code.

At present, our world is going through a period of moral change. Acts once considered virtuous, like propelling an atmosphere-polluting motorboat around a clean-water lake, killing ducks with high-powered rifles will eventually be seen as unhealthily sinful by a large percentage of the population. Other acts determined to be illegally taboo—such as smoking marijuana have already become acceptable to a large percentage of the citizenry.

Consensual Determination

The key issue in an open society is the consensual determination of good and evil, of what is legally moral and illegally immoral. General solutions to this vexing question of moral difference are simple and two-fold:

A. Provide a way of democratically determining, by campaign and vote, the currently acceptable moral codes.

B. Discourage immoral behavior in a socially constructive and psychologically rational way.

Let us define as immoral any behavior physically unhealthy to self, or socially obnoxious to a majority of the citizenry. Let the normal processes of lobbying, public-

opinion persuasion, campaigning, and voting modify the
list of immoral activities and their punishment.

PeNaLTies

Let the social penalty for immoral behavior be
financial, instead of burdening the virtuous tax-
payer with the enormous cost of detecting, arresting, and incarcerating. Let us set a series of special licenses
so that the sensualist, the self-destructive, the unhealthy
are obligated to pay a $1,000 annual contribution to the
social welfare—thereby eliminating irrational guilt and
fear and enormously benefiting the state treasury. Those
who have several vices pay more.

Frivolity Fees

As the saying goes, *"If you want to play, you must
pay the piper."* A few minutes' reflection will
suggest the astounding sums available to the state
treasury from such "Frivolity Fees." For example, the two
million (or more!) marijuana smokers produce profits to
illegal distributors and enormous
drains on the state's treasury. If
only half of the current smokers
decided to purchase a license,
around a billion a year would be
raised.

**Frivolity Fees would
fully fund the
state budget.**

Frivolity Fees will probably turn out to be the only
needed source of state funds. It would be thus possible
to completely eliminate state taxes for the virtuous and,
indeed, to provide rebates and bonuses to the sober and
underprivileged.

IMMORALITY BOUNTY

Any citizen who wishes to indulge in any democratically defined immoral act will be given a Frivolity Tax Card upon which will be punched the particular vices he has paid for. Any person apprehended in an immoral act for which he has no license will pay double—i.e., a $2,000 fine. Fifteen hundred dollars of this fine goes to the state treasury and $500 to the alert arresting officer as an "Immorality Bounty."

If this seems harsh, the convicted sinner can choose the old imprisonment system. Our program is voluntary and requires no revision of the present legal structure. A thief or unlicensed marijuana smoker, for example, can opt to be punished under the old system, or "pay off" his crime under the new system.

WIN-WIN ENFORCEMENT

Bounty payments for the detection and arrest of unlicensed financial and moral culprits will make the police into genial umpires in a good-humored game of dictated order. Under our administration, the alert state policeman will make more money than the current governor's salary. The demand for police jobs will become so great that after a policeman has made enough bounty money to guarantee him lifelong income, he will be retired. Eagerly awaited openings in the police ranks will be filled by firemen.

SIN MONEY

We shall allow the frivolous and dishonest to pay all of the cost of the state government and relieve the burden on the hard-working conservative. But how will the convicted larcenist or the unlicensed immoralist get the money to pay his fines?

> **Police would become genial umpires in a good-humored game of dictated order.**

The State Correction Department will concentrate solely on getting good jobs for those who owe the state "greed" or "sin" money.

Instead of a socialistic system of incarceration and welfare payments, the state will do everything to give "debtors" the chance to work in an interesting and challenging job to "pay off" their crimes. Eventually, most all politicians will be rehabilitated crooks—which, come to think of it is better than the present situation, where most politicians are unrehabilitated crooks.

14

HIP MEETS BEAT

I'LL NEVER FORGET the first time I saw California—in 1946, just after my discharge from World War II service. We had driven down from Oregon through the northern California mountain valleys, past Shasta, along the vineyard trail. To my New England brain the notion of vine-yards sounded like sunny heaven   and then that first unforgettable view of San Francisco from Marin County, with the Golden Gate Bridge soaring across the bay.

Thirty years later, ethology and sociobiology helped us understand the importance of neurogeography—where you are determines which circuits of your brain are activated. When the salmon reaches the special breeding pool, 500 miles up the tributaries of the Columbia River, then the salmon boy-girl light flashes. This is the place! We have arrived in the right ecological niche!

SUNSHINE MISSIONS
TO BACK EAST

I thought of my visits "back East" as Time
Traveler Red Cross Missions—zooming back to
Washington, D.C., or the seething warrens of
the jittery Oriental masses in New York. Every time I
visited the hive-city of Manhattan, I saw it like a trip
down into the Soviet Union—smuggling in hope and
sunny messages from the Far Indies.

In the late sixties, the *East Village Other* was the
leading counterculture voice of the Far East Coast. Like
an 18th Century publica-
tion, they wallowed in
pessimistic and violent
rhetoric. They assumed
the role of victim as
easily as putting on a
comfortable old shoe. So when the *East Village Other*
invited me to Manhattan for an interview, I thought of
it as a kind of mission. I was a hope fiend and I felt it
my duty to unload as much sunny enthusiasm as possible from the Western Future to the Eastern Passed.
And after all, those were the days of flower children
and I was their pied piper.

**As a hope fiend, it's my duty
to unload sunny enthusiasm
on the pessimistic.**

HE SET A
VICTIM TONE

Naturally, the *East Village Other* journalist
opened the interview with the somber question
to set a victim tone. Looking extremely serious,

he asked, *"Have you detected any change in the police harassment you have been subjected to over the last six years?"*

I answered that Rosemary, 1, and our kids had been hassled incessantly. When cops recognized me on the highway, they pulled us over and searched us. If the government didn't like my lectures or my advocacy of drugs, at any moment, they could pull my bail. It hung over my head that I could be locked up at any moment.

I explained that there had been brief a cessation of this persecution when I was running for the highest office in the State of California. During that period any policeman in California was likely to be my assistant in maintaining harmony. For example, just the week prior to the interview I had been in Miami to give a patriotic lecture at a rock concert. At 5 A.M. on our way to our motel, we were pulled over by a police cruiser. Within 2 minutes the captain, and what must have been a large part of the force showed up. This was obviously a little adventure for them. They ran a make on me, and when it was reported that I was Timothy Leary, candidate for Governor of California there was great rejoicing and amusement at headquarters. This encounter ended in a very friendly conversation, in the course of which I offered all the policemen I'd met jobs in California because they were all so alert and good humored.

I told the *East Village Other* journalist that I hoped this atmosphere of reconciliation would continue. He gave me a look that could only be described as "clueless."

PeOPLe's PaRK

Next, the journalist wanted my views on People's Park in Berkeley. I explained that Rosemary and I lived in Berkeley, and were very close to the people masterminding the People's Park incident. I said that I saw it as the classic, perfect example of how to run a psychedelic guerilla campaign.

They lured the university administration, the police, and the National Guard off the campus. There was no issue of seizing buildings. It was simply Cops vs. Flowers, brilliantly conceived and the most effective political event in years.

Cops vs. Flowers! It was brilliant.

When the National Guard helicopter gassed the campus, very few dissenters were hit. They gassed the students in the cafeteria, the ones on their way to classes and patients in the university hospital. They gassed the gym too, which in turn angered the jocks. Anytime you get the jocks running into the streets shaking their fists at the police, you score a victory.

is every COP a PiG?

Satisfied that we were on the same page, the journalist wanted to know if I considered every cop to be a pig. *"Everyone has to do what their karma directs,"* I answered in high hippy style (pun intended!).

There are some people whose karma it is to call cops "pigs", and some engage in violent confrontations. Police and protestors are both playing necessary parts in the drama to show the world how ridiculous the American political and law-enforcement situation is.

But there are others whose karma it is to harmonize. I am a Libra and so I am far from having any interest in inflicting injury. My number one priority is to reward the police. Our country has been engaged in a convulsive punishment experiment. We all know that hitting kids on the head, shooting down dissenters, or gassing students has never worked as a political technique. In my utopian society, we will see to it that the police will be relieved of the tremendous unpopularity now generated by their enforcing laws about morals.

Marijuana Tax

With eyes glassed over, the beatnik journalist was unimpressed with my utopian vision. Instead, he wanted to know if I thought it an injustice to level a tax on grass smokers to alleviate the tax burden of the right wing.

Most pot smokers would rather pay a tax than risk getting busted.

"You have to be practical about this," I cautioned. Most marijuana smokers will pay a tax rather than run the risk of getting busted, which costs considerably more and often involves imprisonment Anyway you look at it, my utopian plan is more beneficial for everybody concerned. Liquor, nicotine, and entertainment are heavily taxed. Why not marijuana, too?

CAMPUS UNREST

Next, my beat inquisitor turned to asking my opinion on the unrest we were seeing across the country. I explained that there is an absolutely foolproof solution for the college and university problem—pull the government out of education! Turn the colleges and universities over to private groups of students and professors to run their own education as they see fit. If the students have complaints against their professors, consider it a trade union problem. Such disputes should be ironed out amongst themselves.

> **With a violent confrontation, we lose in every way.**

The state has no business having anything to say about education other than supporting it with tax subsidies. Education should be free of government interference. Of course, one of our major efforts should be to cut down burgeoning state bureaucracy, which plagues all of us. Prison population should be cut by at least 90%. Only those who insist on being violent should be kept behind bars.

THE CHICAGO 8

"The Trial of the Chicago 8 was perfect!" I told the journalist. Mayor Daley was sent down to play his part in the genetic plan to free us all.

The revolution is hedonic. The key is internal freedom that goes beyond classes. What impressed me at the time was that when you visited the most deserted parts of the country, you found the kids were most outspoken. They may not have considered themselves revolutionists at all, but they were completely disgusted with the establishment.

Anyone who speaks to students honestly about individual freedom receives their full-scale support. Until the moment of my death I remained popular among college students. Young people lounging on my deathbed surrounded me. I believe that my attraction was being honest about individual freedom.

The violent confrontation in Chicago resulted in 70% of the American people siding with Mayor Daley. That shows that confrontation, while necessary, was essentially a setback. On the other hand, the People's Park issue in Berkeley, where the issue was planting grass and beautifying a dump, resulted in a 66-to-1-vote of confidence by the student body. By provoking a confrontation in which we are righteously joyous, we won 89% of the young and over 50% of the older. There is a critical message here.

With a violent confrontation, we lose in every way. There is no question about the revolution being won through the spirit of the West Coast, which is the spirit of confidence, the certainty that hedonic tactics and pleasure guerrillas will win out. The average high-school kid does not want to carry arms, he wants to get high and fuck in a spiritual manner. Kids laugh at violent politicians. I agree with them.

The politics of violence is futile. You are never going to win anyone over by being uptight. A frowning face with lips pursed like a hen's asshole does not melt hearts. Take Berkeley. After the murder of a young man by the police, the gassing of the campus by the National Guard, and a series of threats, our reaction was flowers. Let's face it, violence on both sides comes from violent heads whose future is inevitably doomed.

AND
PORNO?

The key energy for an utopian revolution is
erotic I told the beat journalist. A free person is
one whose erotic energy has been liberated and
can be expressed in increasingly more beautiful, complex ways. Wilhelm Reich said it first.

The sexual revolution is the center of the free
atmosphere generating within the kids. Psychedelic
drugs, particularly marijuana, are popular because they
turn on the body. The central issue of the psychedelic
experiences is the erotic exhilaration.

The increased freedom of sexual expression in art
and mass media was symptom number one of our
victory back in the sixties. On the West Coast, 12-year-
old kids were fucking righteously and without guilt,
very poetically. The average 15-year-old had explored
most single and many multiple ways of sexual expression and was ready to go to a more spiritual Tantric
path.

In an interview in *Look* circa 1969, a 17-year-old
girl was quoted as saying that grass was great for balling.
To which *Look*'s middle-aged expert said in a pitying
way, *"What does she know about sexual intercourse?"* It
showed the key to the generational gap. Most 17-year-
olds have had orgasms longer, deeper, and more complex than their ancestors. The older generation just
can't stand this, and therefore repress it.

15

CAMPAIGN BLOCKED

PLANS TO MAKE THE MOVIE and win the California election were easily blocked. Two weeks before the filing date for candidates, one of my rivals visited a Hollywood movie producer who had contributed generously to former Democratic campaigns. The producer refused to give a contribution because he was "waiting to see how the Timothy Leary campaign was developing." My rival blanched and blurted *"Shit, you're the fourth Hollywood Democrat to tell me that in two days. This joke has to stop."*

> My campaign became an actual threat.

Foreign news coverage of my campaign didn't make American politicians laugh either. The Europeans loved my TV interviews, with catchy lines like *"The function of government is to entertain."* My campaign was becoming an actual threat and my rivals didn't take any chances. One week before filing date for candidates, I was imprisoned without bail. The lawyers had assured me this just couldn't happen in America—but they forgot that Reagan was governor and Nixon was president.

The case against me was flimsy, at best—two roaches and seven marijuana flakes vacuumed from the pocket of a jacket. We had a credible witness to testify that the arresting officer had a history ofusing illegal tactics to get an arrest.

The case against Rosemary and Jack was more substantial. The DA let me know that if I were found innocent he'd go after them with particular vigor. It made sense for me to take the hit. Plus my lawyers were confident that I'd be freed on appeal bond and we'd get my conviction overturned in a higher court. So I went along with their plan of putting up *no defense*.

We were all found guility of possession. Rosemary and Jack got probation. No surprise there. The shock came when the judge read aloud from the *Playboy* article I'd written and then remanded me directly to jail.

The lawyers were helpless. I spent five weeks in solitary confinement waiting for my sentence. I got nearly 20 years in prison for two roaches and a few flakes. It was clearly unconstitutional.

So I was prevented from filing to run for govenor. Instead I spent the primary season in prison, and learned about Ronald Reagan's election from the safety of Algeria, to which I had fled after my escape from prison.

16

EXILE BLUES

THIS IS NO PLACE to discuss my political
adventures in Algeria, Libya, Egypt, and
Lebanon, except to say that Arab Socialism is
a vengeful, violent, barbarian concept that hasn't
changed a microgram since Medina, A.D. 622. There
is no "Politics of Ecstasy" behind the Arab veil.

Algeria, at the time of my exile—and still is—was a
hotbed of intrigue and espionage. Everyone in Algiers
was an agent of one or more political powers, exiled
governments, and liberation fronts. After surveying the
political chessboard, I opted for the most capitalist-
democratic country in
the world, Switzerland.
I tricked the Algerian
government into
issuing exit visas to

**The place reeked of paranoia
and double-agentry.**

attend a Communist convention in Denmark. Then we
jumped the plane in Zurich and applied for political
asylum in Switzerland. After six months, with two
months spent in Bois Mermet prison on an American
extradition warrant, I was given asylum in 1972 under
the condition that I say *nothing* about drugs.

GreeN HeLL

Switzerland is so green and beautiful because it rains, rains, rains in the damp, gloomy Alps, and the sun never dries things out. They called it "the green hell." The Swiss are good people, but soggy and bored. Little scientific work was done. I learned how to ski, wrote some memoirs, produced and sang on a rock 'n' roll record, made a movie, and wallowed in the Exile Blues.

It was not possible for me to discuss the positive benefits of drugs like hashish, LSD, and opium, or to describe the scientific basis upon which I based my belief that these drugs should be legal and freely accessible. I was a scientist who had spent 15 years at that point studying the effects of drugs on human psychology and human behavior, yet I was not allowed to present the results of my research.

For the 10 years, starting at Harvard University, every administrator—and every government official I'd talked to—indicated that I was not allowed the freedom to discuss the reasons why

I was an outlaw and a stateless person.

the laws should be changed. It was a clear violation of the American Constitution, academic freedom, scientific openness, and of all the principles upon which democratic societies are based. At that time—and still today—there is no country in the world in which I, an outlaw and stateless person, would be permitted to pursue my scientific work.

Vienna

In January 1973 I fled to Vienna. The Austrian government had invited me to make an anti-heroin movie. Chancellor Bruno Krelsky said he hoped I could help him bring Austria into the 20th Century. I was feted and treated by Viennese intellectuals, but Austria is darker and damper than Switzerland. The hottest book in Vienna was, at that time— believe it or not—*Das Kapfta!*

Kidnapped in Afghanistan

Heading for the sun of Ceylon, I flew to Beirut. I was welcomed by the dope-oriented Lebanese aristocracy, but the place reeked of paranoia and double-agentry. In Afghanistan, a uniformed official at the Kabul airport requested my passport, and American agents then moved in to bust me for not having a passport.

It was blatant kidnapping. No one noticed. No one protested.

A prince of the royal house said, "*Not to worry, my family will protect you.*" In three days I was escorted by a battalion of armed soldiers to an airplane where American agents waited to take me back to California. It was blatant kidnapping, but no one noticed. Nixon was reinaugurated that month. And there are no lawyers in Afghanistan. The king was overthrown a few weeks after my kidnapping; he had more troubles than I did.

17

THE ESCAPE TRIAL

IN THE SPRING OF 1973, while awaiting my escape trial I was confined to the "hole" of the San Luis Obispo state prison. The California prison officials were very irritated with me. During this period my only human contacts were with other inmates—mostly psychotic murderers—who could be seen and heard through a one-foot window in the iron cell-door. Written contact with the outside world was severely censored.

> Philosophers of freedom have always been brought to trial for being dangerous to the state or corrupting youth.

Finally I was hauled into court to be tried for escape. Security precautions were extravagant. Afraid of another Weatherman coup, five patrol cars escorted me from prison to the courthouse. My lawyers told me to be as far out as possible. It made no difference, because the fact of my escape was undeniable.

QUEEN OF HEARTS COURT

DEFENSE COUNSEL: *In your escape note, you wrote: "In the uniform of Athens you jailed Socrates. In the uniform of Rome you jailed Jesus Christ, and in the livery of Nixon and Reagan you have turned this land into a police state." Could you explain to the jury what you meant by this poem?*

Dr. LEARY: My nervous system is in such a state that I live in many reincarnate levels.

PROSECUTOR: *Objection, Your Honor. Calls for a medical conclusion.*

THE COURT: *Overruled.*

Dr. LEARY: I saw what was happening at the prison on September 12th, 1970—the day of my escape—as recurring events which happen over and over again. We simply play out the same parts. Freedom is always the issue, and philosophers of freedom have always been brought to trial for being dangerous to the state or corrupting youth.

My nervous system, as a result of twelve years of deliberate and disciplined research with drugs and different forms of yoga, allows me to put my mind in different places. My nervous system essentially travels throughout historical time. To become "Timothy Leary" *is like getting in a car and turning the key. I'm not a "Timothy Leary model" most of the time. That's just one small fragment of a nervous system that makes us think we are Catholics or Republicans or Chevrolets or Pontiacs. Actually we can leave the automobile of our present identity and move throughout our nervous system.*

> **I'm not Timothy Leary—
> I just use his identity.**

DEFENSE COUNSE: *Could you explain that in reference to how you felt when you wrote this poem on September 12th?*

DR. LEARY: *Yes. I'm not Timothy Leary most of the time. I use the Timothy Leary identity to move throughout space and time to accomplish my mission and my survival. We are not cars; we use cars. We can step out of cars. You can step out of your historical role and move into any other role.*

DEFENSE COUNSEL: *Had you stepped out of the car when you wrote this poem on September 12th, 1970?*

DR. LEARY: *At the time I was writing this poem, I could just as well have been Socrates, or those people who were burned at the stake in the Middle Ages. I was no more Timothy Leary than I was any of these. People in the future will understand what is happening now just as we understand what happened in Salem 200 years ago.*

PROSECUTOR: *Again, I am going to interpose an objection on the basis of relevancy, Your Honor.*

THE COURT: *Overruled.*

DR. LEARY: *Periods of madness overcome every country at certain points in history, usually during a war. And at these times of hysteria, any voice speaking for the eternal values of freedom tends to get persecuted. Many men who stood up and said, "We shouldn't hang people as witches in Salem," then became accused of being witches. I am in prison because I am considered to have dangerous beliefs.*

Prosecutor: Objection, Your Honor. That answer is not responsive, and self-serving.

The Court: Overruled. That's his conclusion, Counsel.

Defense Counsel: On September 12th, 1970, did you believe you were in prison for your beliefs and not for crimes you had committed?

Dr. Leary: Yes, I did. I believe that no government has the right to interfere with what happens inside someone's body or nervous system. Anything we do behaviorally in public to hurt anybody else in any way, that is a crime. What we do inside our bodies with our nervous systems, or anything that we say in the way of a lecture or writing cannot be punished, as per the First Amendment to the Constitution.

Defense Counsel: Did you believe that you had never done an act that would be objectionable in a behavioral sense?

Dr. Leary: Yes, I did then and do believe today that I have never harmed a hair on anyone's head.

Defense Counsel: Why did you feel that you fit in with that category, Doctor?

Dr. Leary: The judge who remanded me to this prison without bail said openly and publicly that I was to be jailed because of my beliefs, because of my published articles.

Prosecutor: Objection, Your Honor. I ask the answer be stricken as hearsay and self-serving.

THE COURT: *Overruled.*

DEFENSE COUNSEL: *Now, Doctor, the "Eagle Brief" dated September 12th—was it directed at any particular person?*

DR. LEARY: *It was directed towards everyone in our country because if even one person is punished or imprisoned for their beliefs and statements, we are all affected.*

DEFENSE COUNSEL: *Now, you have also put in this poem, "Listen, guards, to this ancient truth. He who enslaves is himself enslaved. The future belongs to the blacks, the browns, the young, the wild and the free." What did you mean by that?*

DR. LEARY: *Well, I believe that the world does belong to the future. I see myself as a person from the future. I like to believe I am from the 21st Century, visiting here to play a historical role, as one would visit a primitive tribe in New Guinea to pass on warnings and counsel.*

DEFENSE COUNSEL: *Now, this poem goes on, "Oh, prison guards, I pray that you will repent and reform." Did you have any animosity to these guards?*

DR. LEARY: *Not at all. I have profound sympathy for them.*

DEFENSE: *"Open the gates of your hearts and be free. Break out. Follow me to freedom, love laughter." Is this an indication that you were going to escape and that they should break out with you?*

PROSECUTOR: *Objection, Your Honor. Leading?*

THE COURT: *Overruled.*

DEFENSE COUNSEL: *Did you want them to follow you out of the California Men's Colony?*

Dr. Leary: *I was talking about the prison of their minds, not specifically the prison at San Luis Obispo.*

Defense Counsel: *Could you be more specific for the benefit of the jury?*

Dr. Leary: *I believe we are imprisoned by the past. It's necessary to escape the shackles of what has happened before if we are going to survive in the future. This particular line is the same message that I have advocated in every page of the many books that I have written: We must free ourselves from the rear view and move to the future.*

Defense Counsel: *Doctor, did you write this letter for an escape note from prison?*

Dr. Leary: *Not specifically. Escape in every way from any sort of confinement which is unhealthy and unjust.*

Defense Counsel: *Did you feel on September 12th that there is something innately important about escape?*

Dr. Leary: *Escape is the message of my life in every form.*

**Escape is the
message of my life.**

Sentenced

I was given five years, consecutive, for the crime of escape! The judge—a crusty, old curmudgeon who had been active in Republican politics for 30 years—died 2 years later. The headline for his obituary in the *L.A. Times* read: "Leary Judge Dies." I thought that was pretty ironic.

QUEEN OF
HEARTS COURT
REDUX

"*Give your evidence,*" said the King; "*and don't be nervous, or I'll have you executed on the spot.*"

"*There's more evidence to come yet, please your Majesty,*" said the White Rabbit jumping up in a great hurry; "*this paper has just been picked up.*"

"What's in it?" said the Queen.

"*I haven't opened it yet,*" said the White Rabbit, "*but it seems to be a letter, written by the prisoner to—to somebody.*"

"*It must have been that,*" said the King, "*unless it was written to nobody, which isn't usual, you know.*"

"Who is it directed to?" said one of the jurymen.

"*It isn't directed at all,*" said the White Rabbit; "*in fact, there's nothing written on the outside.*" He unfolded the paper as he spoke, and added "*It isn't a letter, after all: it's a set of verses.*"

"*Are they in the prisoner's handwriting?*" asked another of the jurymen.

"*No, they're not,*" said the White Rabbit, "*and that's the queerest thing about it.*" (The jury all looked puzzled.)

"*He must have imitated somebody else's hand,*" said the King. (The jury all brightened up again.)

"*Please your Majesty,*" said the Knave, "*I didn't write it, and they can't prove I did: there's no name signed at the end.*"

"*If you didn't sign it,*" said the King, "*that only makes the matter worse. You must have meant some mischief, or else you'd have signed your name like an honest man.*"

There was a general clapping of hands at this: it was the first really clever thing the King had said that day.

"That proves his guilt," said the Queen.

"It proves nothing of the sort!" said Alice. *"Why, you don't even know what they're about!"*

"That's the most important piece of evidence we've heard yet," said the King, rubbing his hands; *"so now let the jury—"*

"If any one of them can explain it," said Alice, (she had grown so large in the last few minutes that she wasn't a bit afraid of interrupting him,) *"I'll give him sixpence. I don't believe there's an atom of meaning in it."*

The jury all wrote down on their slates, *"She doesn't believe there's an atom of meaning in it,"* but none of them attempted to explain the paper.

"If there's no meaning in it," said the King, *"that saves a world of trouble, you know, as we needn't try to find any. And yet I don't know,"* he went on, spreading out the verses on his knee, and looking at them with one eye; *"I seem to see some meaning in them, after all. '—said I could not swim—' " You can't swim, can you?"* he added, turning to the Knave.

"No, no!" said the Queen. *"Sentence first—verdict afterwards."*

"Stuff and nonsense!" said Alice loudly. *"The idea having the sentence first!"*

"Hold your tongue!" said the Queen, turning purple.

"I won't!" said Alice.

"Off with her head!" the Queen shouted at the top of her voice. Nobody moved.

—Alice in Wonderland
from the original edition

18

INTELLECTUALLY PRODUCTIVE PERIOD

AFTER THE ESCAPE TRIAL, I was shipped to Folsom—the deepest, darkest pit in the California correctional system. The probation division of the California prison system is called, believe it or not, "the Adult Authority".

I WROTE WITH A PENCIL STUB

I wrote continually during this period. I published hundreds of interviews and articles explaining the politics and ethics of brain-chemistry from the time of my conviction in 1966 to my escape-exile in 1970. Writing materials were limited to a pencil stub not long enough to be used as a weapon. My essays were disguised as legal briefs and smuggled out during lawyer visits.

Awaiting trial for my escape, sitting on the floor of the cell, I wrote *Neurologic* on the back of an Angela Davis legal brief, the only paper allowed.

My essays were disguised as legal briefs and smuggled out during lawyer visits.

During that period I was invited by The Forum of Contemporary History to write an essay about the sixties. The essay I wrote while sitting under the naked bulb of the cell with a pencil stub was widely reprinted and served as the script for a television documentary shown on Public Broadcasting stations.

NTra-MaTTress LiBrary SySTeM

At Folsom I was plunged into 4-A, the dread max-max, the prison within a prison, and celled between Charles Manson and Geronlmo, the fiercest militant Black Panther. Later I was placed on the Main Line of Folsom, where I was swept up into the most productive intellectual period of my life.

The prison library was superb. Interlibrary loans made available any book in the world. In addition, the IntraMattress Library System was available. Prisoners secreted contraband books that were loaned for a carton of cigarettes a week and sold off when inmates transferred. There were books on safecracking, alarm systems, key manufacture, bomb building, organic chemistry, and a classic collection of English language pornography equal to that of the Vatican Library.

The research facilities were also excellent. I remember one rainy Saturday afternoon when the yard was closed and I was thus prevented from visiting the library. I was writing *Terra 11*, a space colony text, and needed to know how big a mini-earth should be to handle 500 souls.

So I banged on the bars and shouted out, *"What is the formula for the area of a sphere?"* Within one minute, 3 sources from the 5-tier cell-block shouted down the answer.

19

PRISON IS AN OCCUPATIONAL HAZARD

JOANNA HARCOURT SMITH, who was handling my legal defense, needed a film to show at moneymaking benefits. **Benefits for whom** was never clear, but that's the fate of a prisoner. Prisoner officials, of course, denied her request. Never one to be daunted, Joanna learned that prisoners were allowed to give one interview every six months. So Joanna authorized a television network to come to the prison and tape an interview, on the condition that she would inherit the film.

Were you too far ahead of your time?

Reporting from
Inside Fulsom

I had been lifting weights with the black militants, playing baseball on the white Aryan Brotherhood team, and playing handball with Chicanos. I was deeply tanned and never looked better in my life. So when I was ushered into the prison committee room to sit in front of a camera and talk. I was wearing a gray sweatshirt and grinning with health and vigor.

> **I was deeply tanned, smiling with health and vigor. I never looked better in my life.**

During this interview, behind the camera stood the warden, the captain of the guards, and two members of the goon squad, watching with arms folded. Joanna added some film clips of herself standing in front of the granite towers of the frowning prison. The film looked great! She proceeded to show it in front of audiences across the land, in London, Paris, and Rome. The evolutionary significance of this transmission is not up to my par, but everyone liked a healthy-looking, smiling person talking in an empowered and optimistic way from the bowels of a political prison during the Nixon-Agnew administration.

Who is
Timothy Leary?

I began by telling the viewers that I wanted them to know Timothy Leary—as a person. *"I'm a philosopher-psychologist who has been study-*

ing the nervous system for the last 30 years. I probably know as much about how the nervous system works ... the far galactic outposts of awareness and the range of human experiences, as any scientist around."

The interviewer cut in to point out the obvious discrepancy. "Yes, *but you also happen to be in prison." "Well, yes, that may seem odd,"* I agreed. *"but the best philosophers often end up in prison."* Most of the men I had modeled

But you happen to be in prison, Dr. Leary!

myself after were considered lucky to have gotten away with just being in prison for their ideas....

we Need a New PHILOSOPHY

The philosopher is looking for implications; great questions like where do we come from? Where are we going? I've always been interested in finding ways of using our nervous system as instruments to answer the basic questions of life. Any scientist at the frontier of his science gets to basic mystical and philosophic questions. It's inevitable, and I've accepted that responsibility.

We are on this spaceship Earth—how are we gonna get along with each other? I think we need a new philosophy. We've run out of navigational ideas of how to get the great ship moving in the right direction....

Cutting in with another reality question, the interviewer asked, *"Is that why you haven't been accepted totally, yet? Are you too far ahead of your time?" "Yes,"* I agreed, *" I'm in a kind of a time warp."* I continued to explain that I had certain empirical experimental proof that I'm not entirely wrong, because most everything that I've said has happened. In 1966, in my testimony before Senate committees about how we could avoid a drug problem in this country ... I was almost alone, saying that marijuana should not be criminalized, LSD should be turned over to the government, to be treated like fissionable material. In subsequent years, many very conservative organs like the American Medical Association, the American Psychiatric Association, the American Bar Association, even William F. Buckley— they all came around to positions considered radical in the 1960's.

I Never ADVOCaTeD DrUGs

If they hadn't asked me about drugs, I wouldn't have brought it up. I talk about how we can use our nervous system to make this country a better place—how to reduce crime, that sort of thing. I know I have to answer questions about drugs, because I've been labeled. As they say in prison, "*It's on my jacket.*" But I had no more to do with drug usage than Einstein had to do with the Atomic Bomb. When Einstein got to the heaven his destiny led him, and he

> I had no more to do with drug usage than Einstein had to do with the Atomic Bomb.

began talking about the equations of space-time and the relativity theory, I know that there was a reporter saying *"Yeah, Albert, but what about the Atomic Bomb?"* And he'd say, *"Yeah, it's true. Those crazy kids, got hold of my theories and blew up Nagasaki and Hiroshima. . . ."* So I have to take the responsibility for drugs as one application of the philosophy I've been working on.

I never advocated drugs. I defended different drugs against unscientific charges. But as soon as you say marijuana is not a killer drug, you become an advocate. I realize that maybe a third of the people generally liked me, think I was in prison for my ideas. I think another third disliked me intensely and think I led young people astray. Another third probably couldn't care less. *"You're busy enough with your own lives;"* I told the TV anchor, *"my debate with the government is no concern of yours."* I think very few people have read my books. And once the media lay a label on you that way, it's very hard to fight back....

"I was arrested more than once," I told the anchor. Various government officials claimed I had drugs or marijuana in my possession. But, as a matter of *fact*, I was never been *legitimately* arrested. I was in Fulsom because I was running for governor of California, and I published position papers on how to gradually eliminate taxes, crime, the drug abuse problem, and so forth.

One evening I was in a parked car. A policeman came up to the car, opened the door against my wishes, reached in his pocket and pulled out two half joints I'd never seen before and said, *"You're under arrest."* A year later, an Orange County jury believed the policeman's story and found me guilty of possession. Then the judge, instead of giving me bail, as I was entitled to for appeal, held up a book that I had been writing, and said *"Your ideas are dangerous, and we're going to put you in prison to keep you quiet."*

If another middle-aged, middle-class person was found with two roaches in his pocket, he wouldn't have done prison time. But I'm not complaining. I'd been going around the United States for 10 years, talking and spreading my message.

I am a
HOPE FIEND

Being a hope fiend and an optimist, I smiled at the
camera and said that it was good to have a chance to
lay back for a couple of years and see how well the
opposition was doing. Since I had been back in Folsom Prison,
I had two books published. Apparently I was wanted back
here. There weren't very many philosophies of hope and
freedom being broadcast. *"I know it's a risky job,"* I grinned,
"but I'm here and I'm going to keep broadcasting." Hearing this,
the prison warden stomped out of the room.

The TV anchor asked how I was being at Folsom. I
answered that I had had no trouble with prisoners, partly
because my fear index had been pretty burnt out by that time
(with laughter). And in a strange way, Folsom Prison was a
very exciting microcosm. All the problems out there were all
compressed into a little area. *"And if we can learn to get along
here and come out with better ways of doing things ..."*

THEY ALWAYS
ASK ME!

Then the TV anchor cut me off with the question
they *always* eventually ask. *"Even though you say that
LSD is safe, do you think that you've suffered any brain
damage whatsoever?"*

That was a very tricky question for anyone to answer. *"I'm
52. I think that anyone who's still erect after these last five decades
has had his sanity tested."* I had been through a lot of rough
times. My career had been ruined. I'd been in 24 prisons, all
without committing any crime that I know of. In addition, I'd
probably pushed my nervous system as much as any human

being living. I'd taken LSD over 500 times and experienced a wide range of biochemical and neurological possibilities.

   "Is there any objective way to test your sanity?" the anchor persisted. *"Well, people who get to know me seem to think I'm pretty sane. I've written 2 books in the last few months at Folsom.. My book Hope Fiend earned me a quarter of a million-dollar advance, so somebody at Bantam books didn't think it was insane. If I am insane, the government should be happy to let me out and let my insanity be apparent."* I quipped.

> There's an ominous tendency to call "insane" those we don't agree with.

   There's this ominous tendency to call insane anybody that you don't agree with. Before the fall, the Soviet Union put their philosophers and their dissenting poets in an insane asylum. Now, maybe it is insane to hope that something could be done about what's happening in the United States today. But otherwise, make up your own mind.

   "You're a hope fiend?" the anchor asked. I bragged a little. *"Yeah, an irrepressible optimist—the opposite of a repressive pessimist, and I think that's what's running the country today."*

   The film ended with the TV anchor asking me about the significance of a pin on my shirt. I explained that the symbol was a replica of the remnants of a living organism, found on a meteorite. We felt it was proof that life exists somewhere off our planet. And we'd taken this as a symbol of the new philosophy that we were talking about. It contained a figure "8" that represented the infinity sign, implying that the nervous system has an infinity of possibilities.... It kinda ties in that we're visitors on this planet Earth. We're not going to be here very long, we gotta get back in touch with the greater picture. It's a symbol of unity and hope....

20

KIDS AND DRUGS

AS THE FATHER OF TWO CHILDREN, I was as concerned about their education and growth as any parent in the country. I never told my children what to do with their nervous systems, as I never told anyone whether they should or should not take a psychedelic drug. I told what I learned from extensive personal and objective research, about the effects of this wide range of consciousness changing chemicals.

> You can't get kids to do much by coerion or threat.

YOU GOTTA KNOW MORE

Let's face it; there's not much you can do by coercion or threat. And if you are going to try

to teach your kids about psychedelic drugs,
you've got to know a lot more than they do.

If you are concerned about your children's interest
in psychedelics, listen to everything they have to say.
You'll find that they
don't know too much,
because none of us
knows too much
about it. So why don't
you suggest a contract
with your children?
Both try to read

> **Young people today are the most sophisticated, most intelligent, wisest, and holiest generation in history.**

everything you can—pro, con, religious, scientific,
legislative. And at the end of 2 or 3 months, make a
joint decision on the basis of the evidence.

I am very old-fashioned. I would much rather have
my children making these strange explorations with
me. I'm convinced that the present generation of
Americans under twenty-five is the most sophisticated,
most intelligent, wisest, and holiest generation in
history. And by God, they better be.

THE TRUTH SHALL SET ME FREE

I'D LIKE TO DISCUSS MY MOTIVES in talking to the FBI about my escape from prison. Number one, I wanted to get out of prison as quickly as I could. I believed

| I am not a martyr— I am practical. |

that telling the total truth was the best way to get out of prison. I didn't want to continue in a situation where hiding the truth was keeping me in prison. That didn't make any sense to me personally, or philosophically. Secondly, I felt I had a great deal to contribute constructive to activities in the United States of America.

I wanted to use my discussion with the FBI to see if I could work out a collaborative and an intelligent, honorable relationship with different government agencies and law enforcement agencies, and educational agencies. I wasn't turning someone over to The Man just to get out of prison. It was part of a longer-range plan of mine. I was in full possession of my faculties. I thought I could contribute a great deal. I had learned a great deal and I intended to be extremely active in this country in my remaining years, however the things turned out.

I always preferred to work. I never went at it illegally ever again. I preferred to work constructively and collaboratively with intelligence and law enforcement people that were ready to forget the past, and to use me, in the future, because I still had a great deal to say in this country—so I believed. And, in fact, I turned on the heads of a whole new generation of inquiring minds after my final release from prison.

YEP, IT WAS THE WEATHERMEN! SURPRISE! SURPRISE!

FEDERAL AGENT: *Okay, you've probably seen his picture but I'll show it to you again. It's a picture of XXXX. Can you identify that photograph?*

LEARY: *Yes, I believe this is the man who drove the camper from Morrow Bay to San Francisco and from San Francisco to Seattle after my escape in September, 1970.*

FEDERAL AGENT: *When we first started talking about this you said that this is the man who told you that was active in the P.L.*

LEARY: *That's right.*

FeDeraL AGeNT: *You said that he told you that he had acted as a sort of counselor or adviser to the Weather people. Is that, in substance, the conversation you had with him?*

Leary: *Yes, sir.*

I TOLD THeM WHaT EVerYONe ALreaDY KNeW

FeDeraL AGeNT: *Who did most of the planning for your departure in Seattle?*

Leary: XXXX

FeDeraL AGeNT: *What did he do?*

Leary: *Well, we were very busy. They wanted—. There was some talk about making movies so they had a movie maker come up from Berkeley to be with us for about a day, and he brought Berkeley newspapers and he brought San Francisco newspapers.*

Oh yeah, they , they—. I haven't told you this. That night in the—, in the mountains with XXXX, they had me write a little statement thanking the Weathermen for the escape. They said they were going to deliver that in a letter to some Los Angeles and San Francisco newspapers. They were going to use rubber gloves so there would be no

The Weathermen had me write a statement for the press thanking them for my escape.

fingerprints on it, to make public aware of their role in the escape.

FeDeraL AGeNT: *Back to XXXX. According to your account, he seemed to be doing the planning or the discussing or kind of putting it together for your subsequent departure from Seattle.*

LearY: *Yeah.*

FeDeraL AGeNT: *What in substance then, if you recall, did he discuss with you?*

LearY: *Well, the second night, that would be Wednesday night, Wednesday afternoon as well, they had all these identifications and the question was to build up an I.D. so that I could get a passport. Rosemary already had her passport.*

FeDeraL AGeNT: *Under an assumed name?*

LearY: *Yeah.*

FeDeraL AGeNT: *Different name?*

LearY: *Yeah.*

FeDeraL AGeNT: *And the Weathermen had given Rosemary the birth certificate and the necessary documentation for her to get the, her passport?*

FeDeraL AGeNT: *So they were in agreement on that. He considered himself to be just what they considered him to be?*

LearY: *There's no question in my mind.*

FeDeraL AGeNT: *The legitimate—if you can call that legitimate, if you can call it "legitimate" . . .*

LearY: *The above ground.*

FeDeraL AGeNT: *The above ground?*

LearY: *The overground.*

FeDeraL AGeNT: *Yeah.*

Leary: Yes, *because they were . . . . Yeah, it was also settled that— It's hard for me to remember some people. Every time I would see XXXX, he would say, "Your friends send their love." Well, everyone knew. Once I called XXX from Algiers—it would be very easy to trace the date of this because XXXX said, "Heavy weather in San Francisco," and I said, "Oh, Yeah?" He said, "Yeah, they bombed" and was talking about what happened after Cambodia. You see there was continual subtle reference to the Weathermen. It was woven into the texture and fabric of our conversation. He was definitely a conduit from the Weathermen.*

Federal Agent: *Okay. You've mentioned numerous Weathermen so far. Is it correct to assume that each one of them knew your true identity and also that you had just escaped from prison and they were aiding in your escape?*

Leary: *Yes, that's right.*

Federal Agent: *—?? Get*

Federal Agent: *You're positive that everyone that you met, that you described to us so far, was fully aware that they were helping a fugitive escape from prison and they knew who you were? You mentioned that maybe you didn't know until after XXXX left who she was and sthat he was in fact XXXX of the Weathermen. But you're quite sure they knew who you were is that correct?*

No question about it. The Weathermen knew who I was and what they were doing.

Leary: *Oh, no question about it. The Weathermen knew who I was and what they were doing.*

FBI
Summary

No interviews with possible co-conspirators
are set forth at this time because Chicago is
attempting to confirm LEARY's allegations
from non-Weathermen sources. At a future time,
Chicago will set out leads or interview some of these
Weathermen co-conspirators whom Chicago believes
may cooperate, particularly XXXXXXXX and XXXXX
who are apparently settled, no longer directly involved
in Weathermen, and would have the most to lose by
possible conviction and incarceration.

A few of the above leads may appear to have more
Weathermen intelligence value than evidentiary value,
but Chicago believes that they are such an integral part
of this case they should be covered in this caption.
Close coordination between this case and Weathermen/
Weathfug cases is maintained.

Numerous discussions between Chicago Division;
USA, Chicago: and Departmental Attorneys are sum-
marized as follows:

All parties agree that the LEARY interview pro-
vides the basis for some Federal action against culpable
principals and conspirators in this and other matters.
All parties seem equally concerned that substantive
cases be developed which will preclude any criticism of
the Bureau, USA, or Department, especially because of
"political" overtones of case, namely the so-called
persecution of the New-Left by governmental agencies.
Also, other problems include the determination of
which case, or cases provide the best vehicle for pros-

ecution and which venue would be most appropriate,
which decision is apparently to be made by the Department in conjunction with the several USAs involved.
Possibilities for prosecution as discussed include these:

XXX, LEARY, et al Passport Fraud Conspiracy,
venue Chicago

XXX, et al under Accessory after the Fact Statute,
Escape and Rescue Statute (particularly Title 18,
Section 752), and/or Obstruction of Justice.

Separate
Realities
Among Friends

Counter-culture patriots, some who were in
diapers or just a twinkle in their hippy parents'
eyes, are offended that I
talked to the FBI. They
consider telling the Feds
what everyone already
knew—that the Weather-
men had, indeed, master-
minded my stunning escape
and confirming the (false?) identity of the driver—as a
violation of their notion of honor among thieves,
which presumably I was obligated to abide by. Indeed,
some even criticized me for escaping in the first place. I
guess I was expected to be a martyr.

> Would **you** voluntarily
> stay in prison
> —for life—
> for **your** ideas?

Never mind that I am not a thief and was incarcer-
ated for my *ideas*, in violation of my civil rights—and
your civil rights, too, since it is your right to listen to
my ideas, if you so choose. Never mind, that I've never
advocated lying nor made any promises to cover up the

identity of anyone who came to my aid. Never mind
that there's never been any complaint from my rescuers.
Indeed, the Weathermen delivered my statement to the
press and planned to make a movie about the escape
and their triumph over Big Brother. Never mind that
the Weathermen were a terrorist organization—one we
all loved, perhaps—but terrorist nonetheless with all
that that entails.

Twenty-five years later—five years after my death—
my "treason" was exposed. The esteemed *Harper's
Magazine* quoted some of what you read here—reprinted, unquestion-
ingly from the sensa-
tionalism-seeking*
SmokingGun.com—in
a featured box with the
title, "Turn On, Tune

> **One UC Berkeley sociology professor called me a "narcissistic slimeball".**

In, Rat Out!" One UC Berkeley Professor of Sociology
called me a "narcisstic slimeball". It just goes to show
how separate realities can develop—even among
friends.

HISTORY WILL BE THE JUDGE

I was a man in his mid-fifties, facing more
than 25 years in prison for encouraging people
to face up to new options with courage and
intelligence. The American Government was being
run by the likes of Nixon, Agnew, J. Edgar Hoover and
other cynical flounters of individual freedom. We had
just had our trust shaken by the Watergate caper.

* You know how I love sensationalism!

Would you have let men like these keep *you* in prison for life for *your ideas?*

All I had to do was tell them what they already knew. The information was empty. What mattered—and won me my release—is that *I submitted. I bowed to authority.* I am not a martyr. I am practical. There was no question in my mind that it was my duty to get out of prison.

I will let history judge me on this one.

21

COGNITIVE LIBERTY

BY RICHARD GLEN BOIRE, ESQ.

The whole is a riddle, an enigma,
an inexplicable mystery.

—David Hume

READING THE PAGES of *The Politics of PsychoPharmacology*, one glimpses the dilemma of a man who has explored the frontier, crossed the boundary between the tangible and the intangible, and been called before a Goliath government to explain himself, his actions, and what he has seen beyond the horizon.

How does one explain colors to someone who has only seen in black and white? And, what does one do when the monochromatic has been codified into law, and seeing colors decreed a criminal offense?

While most would like to think that the United States has no state religion, no compulsory cosmology, no mandatory worldview, the millions of Americans who have tasted the forbidden fruit known as "psychedelics," "entheogens," and "empathogens," would beg to differ.

Leary was called before a Goliath government to explain himself, his actions, and what he saw beyond the horizon.

A MODERN DAY RELIGIOUS WAR

The war on visionary plants and substances is a modern day religious war—one that is disguised as a "war on drugs," when it is actually a war on certain mental states that allow one to conceive of the world in a way that may not comport with dominant models of reality.

What is a religion? Most religions are pre-packaged reality models. A religion, be it Judaism, Islam, Hinduism, Buddhism, or Christianity, operates as a more or less closed system that tells you how reality is structured, what your place is in it, and how you should live.

It is a war on unauthorized mental states.

Religions are ideological. They may not have started out that way, but after they go on for several thousand years, they seem to ossify, calcify, or harden-up into fortresses of belief. People enter into these fortresses, find security within them, and then defend them against all outsiders.

What any person calls his or her "religion" is an internalized worldview, a personal cosmology or belief system about reality, which is usually shared with others. Once you get enough people together who share a similar belief system, or reality model, you get organized religions.

The "war on drugs" is a misnomer—it's more than a misnomer, it's a strategic attempt to remove the focus from the actual issue, which is *consciousness* itself. Specifically targeted is consciousness that disrupts the confines of cultural programming about how reality "really is." The so-called "drug war" is not a war on pills, powders and plants—it is a war on *unauthorized mental states*.

You won't see it reported this way by the major news networks, or addressed this way by the Drug Czar or the Chief of the DEA, but there is a battle going on right now: a battle over consciousness. How much we can attain, and what form it can take.

MaNTaN THE STaTUS QUO

The government and mainstream culture are all about *maintaining* an established status quo. They want consciousness to remain as static, as steady, as possible. They want to be in control of consciousness. The idea of people turning off their TV sets, escaping their programming, or God forbid, freely manipulating their own consciousness, scares the hell out of the govern-

> A belief is what you hold onto once you've stopped thinking and reached a conclusion.

ment and the globalized corporations that fund it. Seizing control of your own consciousness—your own mental processes—is today's heresy. In fact, the term "heresy" originally meant a belief that one arrived at by oneself (Greek *hairesis*, "choosing for oneself").

Various religions or views of Reality can be analogized to computer operating s-ystems. They are like software for the brain—a sort of reality positioning system. Your view of reality will be affected depending on whether you are running the software or brainware system Catholicism version 3.1, Islam version 2.0, New Age 1.0, or Atheism 2.0. Any of these operating systems will overlay on Reality-at-Large and present you with a graphical user interface of Reality. Load a new operating system into your brain—a particular religion, philosophy, or worldview—and you may not change Reality-at-Large, but you do change how you model reality inside your brain.

> **Faith is something you grasp onto when you have little or no evidence to support a belief.**

Most people, once they learn a particular operating system, develop an allegiance to it that makes it very hard to try a different operating system. We can see this in the computer world with respect to Macs versus PC's and with respect to Windows operating systems versus Linux. Mac users seem to despise PC users and many would never consider switching over to a PC, and vice versa.

WHaT ArE ENTHEOGENS?

Entheogens are more than just another operating system. Entheogens, themselves, come with no dogma, no holy book that one can consult to find the rules for living. Entheogens reveal that *all* belief systems are systems of frozen thought.

A belief is what you hold onto once you've *stopped* thinking about something, once you've reached a conclusion. In the same way, faith is something you grasp onto when you have little or no evidence to support a particular conclusion (or belief) that you have become committed to. Both faith and belief are central to most religions today.

Where religions rely on belief and faith and dogma, Entheogens dispose of belief, faith and dogma, replacing them with a shape-shifting, ineffable, unspeakable, nonsymbolic, experience of reality. Quite literally, you make of it what you will.

ZerO-TOLEraNcE

The US Government has gone so far as to call its drug policy one of "zero-tolerance." The goal for the US government is a "drug free" world (of course they ignore alcohol and nicotine, and pharmaceuticals) and it's not only sending agents all over the world to try and combat drugs it's also bioengineering special breeds of fungus that can be unleashed in *other* countries to destroy "evil" plants such as cannabis, opium poppies and coca plants. The concept of "zero-

tolerance" is a return to the sort of religious intol-
erance that has produced so many religious wars
and conflicts in the past. And we see it very
clearly with the so-called "war on drugs."

So this is a not a "drug war"—at least not in its
most fundamental essence. To say that the "war on
drugs" is a war on *drugs*—on the pills and powders
and plants—is like saying that book burnings and
censorship are attacks on paper and ink, when
actually it is the *ideas* of the writers that are under
attack —that are being suppressed. The so-called
"war on drugs" is a religious war, a war on how we
are permitted to perceive reality, a war on consciousness itself. A war on what kinds of thinking
and awareness are to
be tolerated by the
dominant power and
what types of thinking
and awareness are to
be destroyed, by what-
ever means possible.

Without the right to control your own mind, what freedom remains?

The politics of psychopharmacology have not
changed much in the past forty years. The
marbled halls of power, the columned edifices of
the Establishment, still operate under the pretext
that they have the power to control the Reality
Studio, that consciousness can be cajoled into
narrow corridors. But millions of people in the US
alone have slipped passed the guardian's gates.
Millions of people believe in the authenticity of
their own experiences. Millions of people know
that *they* hold the keys to the Reality Studio.

A NEW MOVEMENT

The last century has seen significant advances in civil rights, women's rights, gay and lesbian rights, and ecological awareness. The coming decades will see the rise of a new social movement, one focused on cognitive liberty, or freedom of thought. A new movement based on the fundamental right of each human being to think independently, to create his or her own reality models, to use the full spectrum of his or her own mind, and to occasion multiple modes of thought and alternative states of consciousness.

Without the right to control your own mind, what freedom remains?

—Richard Glen Boire

Author: *Marijuana Law*
Sacred Mushrooms & The Law
Founder: Alchemind Society
Journal of Cognitive Liberties
www.alchemind.org